Twayne's United States Authors Series

Sylvia E. Bowman, *Editor*

INDIANA UNIVERSITY

James Branch Cabell

JAMES BRANCH CABELL

by JOE LEE DAVIS

University of Michigan

 21

Twayne Publishers, Inc.   ::   New York

MANUFACTURED IN THE UNITED STATES OF AMERICA BY
UNITED PRINTING SERVICES, INC.
NEW HAVEN, CONN.

To
VIRGINIA ANSON MORRIS

Preface

CABELL'S reputation bizarrely illustrates the treachery of literary fame—the unpredictability of both critical and popular taste. From the middle of the Yellow Nineties or Mauve Decade to the end of World War I, he was published regularly, his magazine pieces duly appearing in book form.[1] His audience remained small, his reviewers hostile. Although both the aging Mark Twain and the rampaging Theodore Roosevelt praised *The Line of Love*,[2] the prevailing newspaper view of this and later Cabell volumes was that their chief merit consisted in being illustrated by Howard Pyle.[3] For those who liked "realism," they were too "romantic." For the devotees of "romance," they were too stylized and intellectual.

Then came the suppression, trial, and exoneration of *Jurgen*. Readers primed by the climate of the early 1920's to regard the bootleg risqué as an indispensable element of fine literature— as well as critics whose stock and trade were the baiting of the Puritan and the Philistine and the unearthing of buried Titans —transmuted overnight the hitherto obscure Virginian fantasist into the decade's image of the major writer.

Jurgen ran through many editions. Other Cabell books—both new and reissued—sold fairly well. In magazine essays, book-length critical studies, literary histories, symposia, and anthologies, Cabell found himself elevated to the rank of a "classic" and an "exotic" in the movement of spiritual liberation led by H. L. Mencken, Theodore Dreiser, Eugene O'Neill, and Sinclair Lewis.[4] The latter, in his Nobel Prize Address of 1930, went so far as to name Cabell along with these others—and also with the young Ernest Hemingway and the young William Faulkner—as deserving the attention of the Swedish Academy.[5]

All this pother pleased but did not entirely beguile the skeptical Cabell. Irked by the complaints of reviewers that each work of fiction he wrote after *Jurgen* was either too much like it or fell too far short of it,[6] he suspected that what eminence he had won was largely due to his notoriety as a "sexy" writer whose shock was at once muffled and intensified by *double-entendre,* innuendo, anagram, and allegory.

This suspicion led him not only to predict early his forthcoming obsolescence[7] but, at the same time, to attempt to forestall it by going beyond *Jurgen* in the manipulation of veiled salacity. *Something About Eve,* for example, subtitled *A Comedy of Fig-Leaves,* contains that outrageous chapter "The Holy Nose of Lytreia." And *Smirt,* whose title alliterates with "smirk" and rhymes with "dirt," impudently flaunts them both in the chapter called "The Blonde Princess."

Such devices, however, did not avail to forestall the obsolescence he predicted. Perhaps they even helped hasten it. Critical schools hostile to one or another aspect of Cabell's work successively dominated the literary scene. The neo-humanists, making a fetish of the ethical judgment, disliked both his aestheticism and his lubricity. The Marxists, committed to a sociological variant of the ethical judgment, damned him as an escapist, a reactionary, and a downright fraud. The neo-nationalists of the World War II period dismissed him as one of the "irresponsibles."[8]

Southern "new critics," although reviving the aesthetic judgment, so grounded it in their version of the seventeenth-century Metaphysicals and in an agrarian socio-religious utopian traditionalism[9] as to be cool toward Cabell's peculiar blend of neo-classical satire, romantic irony, and the kind of "modernism" associated with Shaw and Mencken. As for the "newer" or "myth critics," who ought to take an interest in a writer as concerned with myth and symbol as Cabell was from the outset, he has thus far failed to draw them. Either they haven't read him or they are repelled by his sovereign contempt for all the varieties of psychoanalysis on which they rely.

Cabell's abandonment of his principal fictive world of Poictesme for other and lesser countries of the imagination; his tendency to turn from fiction to the essay; above all, his dropping of the name "James" so that he appeared for a while to be a mere "Branch" or offshoot of his former self—these high jinks helped to deplete further his steadily shrinking audience.

Shortly before his death in 1958, a Cabell revival threatened. It was a period of revival, under academic sponsorship, of Henry James, F. Scott Fitzgerald, Nathanael West, to name but a few. Also, the 1920's were staging a comeback among students of

American culture and in the mass media. But even such respected
critics and literary historians as Edward Wagenknecht, Edd Winfield Parks, and Edmund Wilson—despite the excellence of their
re-evaluations—proved unsuccessful in really reopening the Cabell
case.[10] Perhaps the sum of their accomplishment was the guid-
ance or titillation of a few graduate students looking for term-
paper and dissertation topics.

As this study goes to press, most of Cabell's fifty-odd books
are out of print. Even the availability of *Jurgen* in reprints has
been intermittent and precarious. The massive standard treatise
on the decade that was once called "The James Branch Cabell
Period"[11]—namely, Frederick J. Hoffman's *The Twenties*—indexes
only two very minor references to him. The best recent one-
volume survey of our literature since 1900—Willard Thorp's
American Writing in the Twentieth Century—allows him only
four short paragraphs. These deal mainly with *Jurgen* and find
in it little but a twin appeal to snobbery and sex.[12]

It is a rare anthology of American literature that represents
Cabell. Such an astute historian of Virginia culture as Marshall
W. Fishwick portrays him primarily as an iconoclastic escapee
from this culture still so controlled by its premises as to be
driven and trapped, along with Ellen Glasgow, into mere blind
alleys out of Eden.[13] The wheel has indeed come full circle.

One of the greatest ironies in the turning of this wheel is
that a writer who strove so hard to achieve timelessness and
universality should be so persistently viewed as limited by his
times—the 1920's in particular—and should ultimately be thought
of as the victim of his home environment—Richmond-in-Virginia.
Of course, he asked for it over and yet over again by being too
garrulous about his identification with both. Undoubtedly, full
understanding must take into account such conditioning influ-
ences, but they need not lead to prejudgment of his total achievement before it has been systematically explored with all the
points of view that are at one's critical command and that
appear feasible in the light of the texts.

The present study proposes to conduct such an exploration
and to use it as the basis of a fresh, final judgment. The assumption will be that a writer who has produced such a God's plenty
of idiosyncratic work as Cabell, who has been so highly praised
by a few critics of the very broadest grasp—such as Vernon
Louis Parrington, Joseph Warren Beach, Leon Howard, Albert

Leon Guérard, Carl Van Doren, and Edmund Wilson[14]—and who has been carped at by so many others for such a diversity of reasons, at least possesses complexity.

To show what is involved in this complexity and to find out how coherent its components are and how fraught with permanent human significance—such are the challenges this study proposes to meet. It will present only such biography and other background as are deemed necessary to clear the path to the major and most of the minor works. Biographical information about Cabell, once scarce, will soon be abundant. *Between Friends,* a volume of his and others' letters, 1915-35, edited by Margaret Freeman Cabell and Padraic Colum, has been published by Harcourt, Brace & World, Inc., too recently for use hereinafter. Emmett B. Peter, Jr., of Leesburg, Florida, is bringing to completion a Cabell biography based on much unpublished material and on extensive research in Richmond, Williamsburg, and New York City. Pending the appearance of this work, the student of Cabell who is interested in his biography primarily for the light it can shed on his creative inspiration, intentions, and development must be content with a sketch founded on a few published sources, most of which are Cabell's own writings. Chapter I of this study is such a sketch. Its title, "Education of a Romancer," was suggested by one of Cabell's remarks in *Special Delivery:* "we are all at school every day of our lives. . . ."[15]

Chapter II of the present study attempts to set forth a series of critical perspectives for reinterpreting and re-evaluating as a whole the eighteen volumes of the Storisende Edition of Cabell's *Works,* which he liked to refer to as "Biography of the Life of Manuel" for reasons that will shortly be explained. Chapters III, IV, and V contain more detailed analyses of the various fictions, both long and short, that develop each of the three main themes with which this extended work is concerned—namely, the chivalrous, gallant, and poetic ways of life. Chapter VI discusses in a similarly explicit manner most of Cabell's numerous later writings, especially the trilogies to which he gave the covering titles "Their Lives and Letters," "The Nightmare Has Triplets," "Heirs and Assigns," and "It Happened in Florida." Chapter VII redefines Cabell's place in twentieth-century literature with reference to his entire canon.

Because Cabell inveterately revised his already published books, very much as Henry James and George Moore did theirs,

Preface

the evolution of much of his canon—particularly the "Biography
of the Life of Manuel"—bristles with problems for the special-
ized researcher. The present study eschews these problems
almost altogether to concentrate on thematic and formal analysis
of each of Cabell's sequence works in the shape, and approxi-
mately in the order, their author finally designed them for
reading.

JOE LEE DAVIS

University of Michigan
Ann Arbor

Acknowledgments

My greatest indebtedness is to Margaret Freeman Cabell for permission to quote from (as well as paraphrase and summarize sections of) the following published works by James Branch Cabell to which she holds the copyright: *The Works of James Branch Cabell* (Storisende Edition, 18 volumes), *Some of Us, Preface to the Past, The Witch-Woman, These Restless Heads, Special Delivery, Ladies and Gentlemen, Smirt, Smith, Smire, Hamlet Had an Uncle, The King Was in His Counting House, The First Gentleman of America, There Were Two Pirates, The Devil's Own Dear Son, Let Me Lie, Quiet, Please,* and *As I Remember It.* I also wish to thank Harcourt, Brace & World, Inc., for permission to paraphrase material from pages 130-35 of *The Woman Within* by Ellen Glasgow.

I wish also to make special acknowledgment for permission to quote from the following works still in copyright:

To Margaret Freeman Cabell, A. J. Hanna, and Holt, Rinehart, and Winston, Inc., for permission to quote from *The St. Johns* by Branch Cabell and A. J. Hanna.

To Farrar, Straus & Cudahy, Inc., for adding its permission to Margaret Freeman Cabell's to quote from *The Witch-Woman* and *The Devil's Own Dear Son* by James Branch Cabell.

To Doubleday & Company for adding its permission to Margaret Freeman Cabell's to quote from *Smire* by James Branch Cabell.

To the University of Florida Press for adding its permission to Margaret Freeman Cabell's to quote from *Quiet, Please* by James Branch Cabell.

To Carl Van Vechten and Yale University Library for permission to quote from "Mr. Cabell of Lichfield and Poictesme" in *Fragments from an Unwritten Autobiography* by Carl Van Vechten.

To Northrop Frye and Princeton University Press for permission to quote from *Anatomy of Criticism* by Northrop Frye, copyright 1957, by Princeton University Press.

To Edmund Wilson and *The New Yorker* for permission to

quote from "The James Branch Cabell Case Reopened," in *The New Yorker* for April 21, 1956.

To Theda Kenyon and Julian Messner, Inc., for permission to quote from *The Golden Feather* by Theda Kenyon.

For permission to reproduce the photograph of James Branch Cabell on the jacket of this volume, I wish to thank A. L. Dementi of the Dementi Studio, Richmond, Virginia.

Contents

Chronology

1879   April 14, born in Richmond, Virginia.

1895- Poems—some of which appeared later in *From the Hidden*
1898   *Way*—published in the *William and Mary College Monthly*.

1898   Graduated with high honors from the College of William and Mary, Williamsburg, Virginia, after teaching French and Greek as an upperclassman.

1898- Engaged in newspaper work in Richmond, New York
1901   City, and again in Richmond.

1901   "The Comedies of William Congreve," revision of a paper written in 1895, published in April issue of *International*.

1901- Engaged in genealogical research in America and abroad.
1911

1902   Seven stories published in national magazines.

1904   *The Eagle's Shadow* published.

1905   *The Line of Love* published.

1907   *Branchiana* (genealogy) and *Gallantry* published.

1909   *The Cords of Vanity* and *Chivalry* published.

1911- Worked in coal mines in West Virginia.
1913

1911   *Branch of Abingdon* (genealogy) published.

1913   September, *The Soul of Melicent*—later entitled *Domnei*—published.

1913   November 8, married Priscilla Bradley Shepherd.

1915   *The Rivet in Grandfather's Neck* (completed 1911) and *The Majors and Their Marriages* (genealogy) published.

1915   August 25, Ballard Hartwell—Cabell's son—born.

1916   *The Certain Hour* and *From the Hidden Way* published.

1917   *The Cream of the Jest* published; Burton Rascoe stirs up Cabell controversy in Chicago.

1918 Elected president of the Virginia Writers' Club.

1919- Served as editor for the Virginia War History Commission.
1926

1919 *Beyond Life* and *Jurgen* published; became genealogist of the Virginia Chapter of the Sons of the Revolution.

1920 January 14, *Jurgen* suppressed; *The Judging of Jurgen* published.

1921 *Figures of Earth, Taboo, Joseph Hergesheimer,* and *The Jewel Merchants* published; edited the October, November, and December issues of *The Reviewer,* Richmond's literary magazine.

1922 October 16-19, *Jurgen* exonerated at trial in New York City; *The Lineage of Lichfield* published.

1923 *The High Place* published.

1924 *Straws and Prayer-Books* published.

1926 *The Silver Stallion* and *The Music from Behind the Moon* published.

1927 *Something About Eve* published.

1927- The Storisende Edition of *The Works of James Branch*
1930 *Cabell* published in eighteen volumes, each with a preface.

1928 *The White Robe* and *Ballades from the Hidden Way* published.

1929 *Sonnets from Antan* and *The Way of Ecben* published.

1930 *Between Dawn and Sunrise* (selections, ed. John Macy) and *Some of Us* published.

1932 *These Restless Heads* published.

1932- Served as one of the editors of *The American Spectator.*
1935

1933 *Special Delivery* published.

1934 *Smirt* and *Ladies and Gentlemen* published.

1935 *Smith* published.

1936 *Preface to the Past* published.

1937 *Smire* and *The Nightmare Has Triplets* (brochure) published.

1938   *The King Was in His Counting House* and *Of Ellen Glasgow* published.

1940   *Hamlet Had an Uncle* published.

1942   *The First Gentleman of America* published.

1943   *The St. Johns* (with A. J. Hanna) published.

1946   *There Were Two Pirates* published.

1947   *Let Me Lie* published.

1948   *The Witch-Woman* published.

1949   March 29, Priscilla Bradley Cabell died.

1949   *The Devil's Own Dear Son* (completed November, 1948) published.

1950   June 15, married Margaret Waller Freeman.

1952   *Quiet, Please* published.

1955   *As I Remember It* published.

1958   May 5, died in Richmond, Virginia.

1962   April, *Between Friends* published.

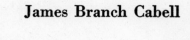

CHAPTER 1

Education of a Romancer

I *Heritage and Boyhood*

JAMES BRANCH CABELL'S paternal grandfather, Robert Gamble Cabell I, son of a governor of Virginia, William H. Cabell, played a minor role in the lives of two of the most famous personages in Virginia's history. He was a fellow student in Richmond of Edgar Allan Poe at the English and Classical School which was presided over by Joseph H. Clarke and later by William Burk. When Poe, in June, 1824, performed the Byronic feat of swimming six miles in the James River, from Ludlam Wharf to Warwick Bar, Robert Cabell accompanied him in a rowboat.[1] Many years later Robert was the next-door neighbor and personal physician of General Robert E. Lee.[2]

To Poe's works, beginning with "The Black Cat," Robert introduced his grandson James at the age of eight.[3] And Robert's reminiscences of General Lee must have afforded this same grandson a unique perspective on the South's most revered chivalrous hero.[4] It is significant that *The Line of Love,* the book from which Cabell says the "Biography of the Life of Manuel" evolved, is dedicated to this paternal grandfather.

James's father, Robert Gamble II, to whom he dedicated *The Certain Hour,* was likewise a physician. James's mother, Anne Branch, to whom he dedicated *Chivalry,* belonged to a family as distinguished as the Cabells. *The Eagle's Shadow* he dedicated to his maternal grandmother, Martha Louise Patteson Branch, who was the model for the delightful grandmother of Jurgen.[5]

Through the marriage of his aunt, Miss Lizzie Cabell, James was cousin to Albert Cabell Ritchie, governor of Maryland for several terms and twice a "dark horse" for the Democratic presidential nomination.[6] Through Anne Branch's sisters' marriages, James was related to such prominent Richmond families as the McAdamses, the Bowies, and the Munfords. One cousin, Thomas Branch McAdams, became president of the American Bankers

Association. Another cousin, the Reverend Walter Russell Bowie, D.D., served as rector of St. Paul's Church, Richmond, and Grace Church, New York City. An uncle, Beverley Bland Munford—eulogized in the poetic dedication of *From the Hidden Way*—was a well-known Virginia lawyer.[7]

The cozy little world into which James was born on April 14, 1879, was benevolently ruled by Mrs. Louisa Nelson, his "mammy," a Negress of some indeterminate age beyond fifty-two, part Indian and part Caucasian, and thrice married. She functioned in all her glory when she sat in Monroe Park in Richmond with other "mammies," in her white cap and large white apron, both befrilled, watching over John's baby carriage while James and Robert played nearby.

These were her "children," dearer to her than her own two daughters, Kizzy and Julia, by her first two husbands. She was the genius of the Cabell household for a quarter of a century, and gave James and his brothers the impression that they were young godlings who could do no wrong and were destined for a special niche in heaven.[8] Since she was thus one of the begetters of Cabell's aristocratic egoism, he quite properly dedicated to her *The Cream of the Jest*.

Among the children's books that nourished the young James's imagination were *Old Greek Stories Simply Told, Stories of Old Rome, Book of Bible Stories*, and—most prized of all—Charles Henry Hanson's *Stories of the Days of King Arthur*, illustrated by Gustave Doré. As the boy relived these stories and listened to his elders talking about the Civil War and Reconstruction, the worlds of the remote legendary past and the recent actual past became strangely confused in his mind.[9]

One elder—reminiscing—reminded him of Ulysses relating his adventures at the court of King Alcinous. Another elder recalled Aeneas entertaining his audience at Carthage. And sometimes their stance and mood suggested the exiles who sat down and wept by the waters of Babylon. General Lee on his horse Traveller was King Arthur riding back from Avalon. Other Confederate generals were Launcelot or Tristram or Gareth or Galahad. Jefferson Davis became Merlin. The Yankees were the legions of the evil Mordred. Carpetbaggers roved the ruined enchanted land like ogres.[10] Thus was born Cabell's profound and abiding sense of the role of myth in human history.

But born with it was a keen sense of irony that was to

grow steadily with the years. Irony is essentially an awareness of the dualisms of experience—the discrepancies in the cosmos, in human nature, and in society. Such characteristics of his environment were soon apparent to Cabell. For, while young James was enthralled by the myth his elders were fashioning to compensate for the South's defeat—even as the Arthuriad grew from the lost cause of the ancient Britons—his sharp senses were daily recording impressions of a modern Richmond that in no way resembled Camelot or Caerleon upon Usk.[11] Furthermore he was quick to note that his elders did not always discourse of their heroes in the same vein.

When these elders climbed on public platforms or rose from ancestral writing desks, solemnity and orotundity possessed them. The past assumed the grandeur of Memorial Day oratory, the dignity of the memoir's rhetoric. But when these same elders were relaxing in the drugstore or the dining room or at the whist table, their anecdotage was more candid and down-to-earth, with occasional touches of malice and scandal, so that the bright armor of this or that member of the Confederate Round Table looked slightly tarnished.[12] It was as if Poe's Imp of the Perverse had got into Ulysses Cabell or Aeneas Branch.

II *Bachelor Years*

As an undergraduate at the College of William and Mary at Williamsburg, Virginia, Cabell was precociously brilliant. A paper he had written in his sophomore year on "The Comedies of William Congreve" had been so impressive that he was persuaded to revise it for publication. As an upperclassman he was hired to teach college courses in French and Greek. Slated for graduation with the highest honors in 1898, he withdrew in protest with two other students, as an unprecedented scandal rocked town and gown.

Ellen Glasgow and her sister Cary were staying that May at the Colonial Inn in Williamsburg. Ellen, who was gathering local color for her novel *The Voice of the People,* heard the full story of the scandal from gossips of the "best families" also staying at the inn.[13] The college authorities and various prominent citizens, according to her account, had forced a middle-aged intellectual of Williamsburg to leave town because he was suspected of carrying on homosexual affairs with students at the college. Invoking the principle of guilt by association, the college authorities then proceeded against all the students who had been his friends. When James was included among these, his mother arrived at the Colonial Inn with an attorney. She was there still when Miss Glasgow was, but the attorney had left, having convinced the authorities that there was not a shred of evidence to convict James of anything but a purely intellectual and literary relationship to the village's alleged Oscar Wilde.

So James was duly graduated with high honors. But for weeks preceding the commencement, he was still under a cloud in the eyes of many of his acquaintances. Living by himself at the college center, he often sat alone on the porch of a tavern across from the Colonial Inn. Finally one afternoon Ellen and Cary, filled with intense feminine sympathy for a victim of the mob spirit, went over to chat with him. Thus began the lifelong friendship between two of Virginia's greatest writers.[14]

The mob spirit, Ellen Glasgow believed, once having made an individual its victim, pursued him relentlessly and struck again. Such a phenomenon was in accord, she thought, with a mysterious tendency toward "eternal recurrence" in the workings of circumstance, in the unfolding patterns of most human lives. This theory received confirmation with a vengeance when another gossip whispered to her on an autumn morning in 1901 that James Branch Cabell had murdered one of his mother's cousins.[15]

Many years later James indicated that the cousin in question—John W. Scott—needed killing but that he himself was not the agent of retribution.[16] Perhaps James had been heard to say something comparable to the first half of this observation before the murder took place. Gossips fancied he was concerned about his mother's friendship with Scott. The finding of the dying Scott on the porch of a home a short distance from the Cabell home was enough to direct suspicion to James. Excitement gripped Richmond for weeks. A Pinkerton detective arrived from New York to help solve the mystery. As his inquiry got nowhere and was in fact abruptly terminated, rumor spread that family pressure had hushed up the whole affair and that James must be guilty. The cloud of this rumor hung over him for many more of his bachelor years. But at last the truth came to light. Brothers of a country girl whom Scott had seduced were said to have been his assailants, although never brought to justice.[17]

The rumor-conjured clouds of homosexuality and homicide must have deeply hurt and angered a spirit so sensitive, intrepid, and aloofly oriented toward ideal ends as Cabell's was. Both desperate and defiant, he lived these bachelor years to the hilt. He was busy at three pursuits—finding a means of livelihood that would not interfere with his creative writing and at the same time might abet or inspire it; keeping at this writing so that it would indeed become a perfect handling of "beautiful happenings";[18] and sowing his wild oats after the fashion of a Restoration truewit, such as Dorimant of Sir George Etherege's *The Man of Mode* or Mirabel of Congreve's *The Way of the World.*

After serving as a copyholder on the Richmond *Times* in 1898, he held jobs on the New York *Herald* from 1899 to 1901 and on the Richmond *News* in 1901. For the next ten years he was a subsidized genealogist examining archives in America, France, Ireland, and England. Out of this research came two privately printed volumes establishing pedigrees for living members of the well-to-do and far-flung Branch family and its collaterals—*Branchiana: A Record of the Branch Family in Virginia* (1907) and *Branch of Abingdon: A Record of the Branch Family in England* (1911). From 1911 to 1913 he worked in coal-mining operations in the mountains of West Virginia.

Authors' vocations and avocations apart from creative writing itself frequently help determine the latter's content and form. Oliver Wendell Holmes's and S. Weir Mitchell's labors as physicians made them pioneers in psychiatric fiction. F. Hopkinson Smith's and Joseph Hergesheimer's work as painters affected the descriptive passages in their novels and short stories. Dreiser's apprenticeship in urban journalism and Steinbeck's dabbling in marine biology account for many aspects of their diverse brands of naturalism. In Cabell's case, genealogical research midwived a cycle of fantastic romances and pointed up some of their distinctive philosophic overtones.

The idea of making most of his characters in this cycle of romances the progeny in a lineage extending from modern Virginia back to such ancestors as Manuel the swineherd and Jurgen the pawnbroker, in the imaginary medieval country of Poictesme, was in large measure genealogically inspired—the creative analogue to his professional tracing of the ramifications of the Branch "lines" as well as to his allied interest in the similarly prolific Cabells and their kin. This tracing—which involved many tedious hours poring over dusty, yellowing records often difficult of access in the most improbable, out-of-the-way places— suggested to his poetic imagination two basic metaphors.[19]

One metaphor was fluvial—the image of the endless flowing of stream into river and of river into ocean. Winds and pebbles fretted the flowing like Time and Chance. The ripples—perpetually rising to the surface, maintaining for a moment their agog identity, and then dissolving into nothingness—were human lives.

The other metaphor was comedic—the image of a vaudeville-like play or skit performed again and again by different troupers in varying costumes on changing stages but remaining always the same in essentials. Its first movement depicted a dream of happiness or pleasure; its second, a striving to realize this dream; its third, either a shrugged-off falling short or a disillusioning attainment of the dream's ultimate emptiness. One *dramatis personae* begot the next with an inveterate repetitive gusto and lustiness. And the same grizzled stagehand—Death—lowered each of the innumerable last curtains.

Genealogical research likewise heightened Cabell's sense of irony to the extreme of diabolism. The genealogist eventually becomes a specialist not only in family trees but also in family evils kept out of public documents though abounding in more private sources of information.[20] As he gleans more and more of these hidden defamatory data, he has the illusion of being possessed by the Devil or some one of the Devil's countless avatars or assistants. He conceives of himself, in short, as Satan's clerk. This illusion of devil-possession is what is meant by the term "diabolism."

This "ism" has played an important role in American literature but so far has received inadequate scholarly attention, except perhaps obliquely in Randall Stewart's *American Literature and Christian Doctrine*. The Puritans wrestled with the Devil in their own psyches, and deplored his presence in Indians as well as in Quakers and other so-called Enthusiasts and Antinomians. To orthodox Christians, the deists seemed possessed by the Devil in their efforts to transform God into an absentee mechanic. Washington Irving, Poe, Hawthorne, and Melville made memorable use of the Devil as characters in their fictions. Emerson relates in "Self-Reliance" how he replied to a critic of his intuitions: ". . . if I am the Devil's child, I will live then from

Education of a Romancer

the Devil."[21] Whitman, in "Chanting the Square Deific," added
Satan to the Trinity. Henry James in *The Turn of the Screw*
and Mark Twain in *The Mysterious Stranger* commemorated
their long trafficking and identification with the Prince of
Darkness, his close relatives, and his demonic incubi and suc-
cubi. As for the contemporary American novel, from William
Faulkner to William Styron, most sane judges now admit that
it has gone absolutely to the Devil.

Cabell's diabolism manifests itself in many ways, as will be
shown later; but its most striking embodiment is the clerk Horvendile, who pops in and out of the Poictesme romances like
the personae of Alfred Hitchcock in his many celluloid chambers
of psychological horror. For the ubiquitous Horvendile, the
ultimate contriver of the Cabellian cosmos and its puppets,[22]
bears a name that alliterates with "horror," rimes with "vile,"
and is an anagram for "Horned evil." He thus clearly symbolizes
Cabell's illusion of devil-possession.[23]

Cabell associated this illusion—as well as its corollary, a restive
sensitiveness to the danger of exorcism—with a curious episode
in his genealogical adventures.[24] One of his remote ancestors,
Sir Richard Cabell of Buckfastleigh, Devon, was born in 1620,
graduated from Balliol College and the Middle Temple, served as
justice of the peace and high sheriff, and sided with the Puritans
during the Parliamentary Wars. At his Brooke Manor he is said
to have dallied with black magic and to have summoned a pack
of hell hounds with which he rode on his black mare over the
moor at midnight. One morning his body was found terribly man-
gled and scorched in places; the throat was ripped wide. Sir
Arthur Conan Doyle based the story of Hugo Baskerville in *The
Hound of the Baskervilles* on that of Sir Richard.

Immediately after Sir Richard Cabell's burial, his restlessness
became so apparent that he was dug up and reburied in holier
precincts. A carefully locked tomb resembling a Chinese pagoda
imprisoned his perturbed remains. Since devil-possession was
supposed to have turned him into a vampire, he was still—so
local rumor held—malevolently and hungrily alive in his pagoda,
as one might easily ascertain by inserting one's forefinger in its
keyhole. Cabell did so and was promptly bitten. The bite
haunted him as a mark of damnation binding him to a hell
where not only the soul of Sir Richard had gone but likewise
the souls of such great lovers in medieval romance as Aucassin

and Nicolette and many another aristocratic minion of the moon.[25]

In the stories Cabell was contributing between 1902 and 1913 to *Argosy, Smart Set, Collier's Weekly, Ainslee's, Lippincott's, Red Book, McBride's, Argonaut,* and—above all—*Harper's Monthly,* such minions of the moon were the actors. They were exponents of chivalry, gallantry, or poetry—attitudes to which their author attached special meanings that will be explained later. Soon they were posturing between book covers in *The Eagle's Shadow, The Line of Love, Gallantry, The Cords of Vanity, Chivalry,* and *The Soul of Melicent.* Cabell's publishers were Doubleday, Page, and Company, Frederick A. Stokes, and—again above all—Harper's.

At first glance many of Cabell's minions—whether moving in medieval Poictesme or less archaic eras of the past, or in relatively modern settings in Virginia or England or on the Continent—did not appear very original. Superficially considered, they had a papier-mâché conventional quality; they were like the manikins who made love, matched wits, exchanged repartee, or crossed rapiers in such best-sellers as Anthony Hope's *The Dolly Dialogues* and *The Prisoner of Zenda* (both 1894), Charles Major's *When Knighthood Was in Flower* (1899), and George Barr McCutcheon's *Graustark* (1901).

But editors like Henry Mills Alden, of *Harper's Monthly,* who prevailed constantly on Cabell to bowdlerize his work so that it would not offend the moral notions of respectable subscribers of the Age of Innocence, knew better. The artist Howard Pyle, who was in love with a purified pre-Raphaelite version of the Middle Ages he thought to be historically accurate, and who read carefully every work of fiction he was commissioned to illustrate, also knew better. To him, both the behavior and the sentiments of Cabell's minions seemed oddly and anachronistically off-color now and then, even when their creator had made Alden's recommended revisions. So eventually Pyle asked to be relieved of any obligation to waste his fine talents further on stuff half-true, and so flagrantly in violation of ethical and aesthetic conventions—the papier-mâché formulae insuring permanent value—as this fellow Cabell persisted in composing.

Harper's forthwith dropped Cabell from its list of authors. What may then have appeared a severe blow to his ambitions as a creative writer proved presently to be a boon. Neither

Alden nor Pyle nor many of the respectable subscribers had ever really appreciated his nuances and distinctions as a stylist or a thinker. The world, the flesh, and the devil—had he continued to write fiction for Harper's list or *Harper's Monthly*—would have gradually ceased to give the dream its resonance and reality.[26]

Now he would write as he wished. Editors, publishers, illustrators, and respectable subscribers—the servitors of Mrs. Grundy[27]—could be damned! The peculiar glaze and fillip of his prose would eventually tell, would set him apart from the run-of-the-mill peddlers of rococo piffle, and would put him in a class with such masters as Robert Louis Stevenson, Samuel Butler, Maurice Hewlett, and Arthur Machen. And perhaps someday he would bring to completion a romance worth mentioning in the same breath with that well-nigh perfect exemplar of the genre, Thackeray's *Henry Esmond*.[28]

Dedication to art, however, always clashed in Cabell's psyche with the urge toward more tangible, less spiritual, less intellectual pleasures. In the first chapter of *Something About Eve*, the preternatural Sylvan views with a kind of pitying contempt the antics of young Gerald Musgrave in the throes of creative writing. Beyond the book-laden study where he fidgets at his self-imposed, absurd task is a late April world rich in sensuous and sensual inducements.[29] "Art, Beauty, and Balderdash," one of the epistles of *Special Delivery*, brutally manhandles the notion—dear to disciples of Walter Pater and Oscar Wilde—that aesthetic experience is superior in engrossment and excitement to "the great animal commonplaces" of actual living.[30]

First among such commonplaces for Cabell were the usual diversions of ebullient bachelorhood. The tavern, the bedroom, and the secluded dell lured him away from the library. When he vacationed at one of Virginia's mountain springs, he put a bookish hedonism to the pragmatic test. These springs were resorts where the gentry of several states, usually eastern or southern, congregated in family groups for health, relaxation, and matchmaking during summers and at other suitable seasons. Large cottages, often of brick or stone, with hammock-hung wide porches, formed semicircular rows or other designs stretching away from a many-verandahed, several-storied central hotel, with spacious dining rooms, ballrooms, and bar. Lakes, bathhouses, ornamental summerhouses, enclosed sulphur waters, tennis courts, trim croquet pleasances, and even grottoes with an echo dotted the sprawling park-like grounds, where symmetrically placed trees and shrubs provided vistas and alcoves. Wooded hills rose roundabout billowing away into the blue and hazy distance.[31]

The life led at these springs during most of the nineteenth century and in the earlier years of the twentieth century constituted a bizarre chapter in the saga of American society. The urbanity and gayety of the court of Charles II or of eighteenth-century Bath flourished anew in surroundings more picturesque and atmospheres uniquely bracing and robust.

Back in the 1830's, at White Sulphur Springs, the largest and most popular of these resorts, the wife of Judge William Cabell wrote a predominantly anapestic poem in fourteen quatrains to the current arbiter of the spa's festivities, fashions, and decorums—Col. William Pope from Alabama. Marriage and money, beaux and belles, servants running, cotillions and waltzes, the soft voices of songstresses, and quaffing at the cool, limpid fountains as a cure for every ill that e'er worried flesh or tormented bone—these are among the motifs featured in her lilting lines.[32]

The resort favored by bachelor Cabell in his libertine twenties and early thirties was the Rockbridge Alum. It ran White Sulphur Springs a close second in size, popularity, and the latest fads in color schemes for everything from bedspreads and window drapes to cake icings. The management catered especially to business and professional men and their families.[33]

One "come-on" included the following sentence: "The place offers as good an opening as can be found anywhere in the mountains of Virginia for such of our young ladies as desire clever husbands."[34] Cabell later reported that its waters were supposed to have had an aphrodisiac effect on the gentler sex. He wondered whether another of the effects was not the kind of light forgetfulness that outfoxes conscience, flouts fidelity, facilitates terminations, and sanctifies hypocrisy.[35]

If the exploits and attachments of Lee and his generals, as told about by Cabell's elders, had made vivid to him a lost world of chivalry reminiscent of Malory's *Le Morte d'Arthur*, the purlieus, habitués, and diversions of the Rockbridge Alum—as he came to know them season after season—composed a world of gallantry that would soon be lost as well; but for the moment it was pulsatingly alive and suggested a comic extravaganza co-

produced by Thomas Nelson Page and Casanova.[36] Ready-made
for Cabell was the world of *Jurgen*, down to the last bush, cave,
mist-tatter, and hamadryad. Here he found settings, characters,
and episodes for many of his other stories also—both of Poictesme
and elsewhere.[37]

Perhaps Cabell's diabolism, growing gamey with age, caused
him to exaggerate in *These Restless Heads* and even more so in
Quiet, Please and *As I Remember It* not only the number of
seductions and adulteries that took place behind the Alum's
façade of respectability, but also the extent of his personal par-
ticipation in such illicit amours both at the Alum and in other
places. Taking him at his word, one can say in partial extenua-
tion of his conduct that he was merely following the code of
young southern males of his time and class. It was a code governed by "the double standard,"[38] one of whose several odd
tenets was that women were divisible into two definite categories
—the worshiped and the wanton.

Those in the first category were ensconced—at least for whatever interval they permitted attention—upon a kind of Platonic
pedestal, for chivalry's chaste perusal. Those in the second category—until they tired of one, or one tired of them—were tum-
bled upon more recumbent accommodations than pedestals, as
the spoil of gallantry's hot chase. Occasionally the neophytic
male, trying ardently to put the double standard into practice,
crossed up his lines and fell chivalrously in love with a wanton
who jilted him cruelly, as Cressida did Troilus—and as Dorothy
la Désirée did Jurgen.

Something of this sort also happened to the young Cabell
early in his career at the Rockbridge Alum. Thereafter he ab-
jured love and sought opportunities for the indulgence of what
might more candidly be called lust. His co-partners in such
affairs, according to his claim, were somewhat numerous for
the next twelve years. In his account, neither they nor the affairs
—as some of his readers might be prone to conclude—were mere
figments of the genealogical or the poetic imagination. But each
affair, he also claims, was managed discreetly, with no unpleas-
ant consequences to anyone but with great benefit to the "Biography of the Life of Manuel."[39]

Finally, on an at once blessed and fatal late afternoon in the
summer of 1912, Cabell walked out on a platform in front of
the central hotel of the Rockbridge Alum and noted the unusual

profile of a woman sitting alone on the trellised porch of the fifth cottage of the row to his right. This was Mrs. Emmett A. Shepherd, the widow of a late lumber merchant of Richmond, formerly Rebecca Priscilla Bradley, nicknamed "Percie," of Charles City County, Virginia. Her five children by her deceased husband—one son and four daughters, the eldest of whom, Isabelle, her first-born child, was a virtually helpless and witless victim of infantile paralysis—needed a father.

Drawn by facets of Mrs. Shepherd's personality and character as unusual as her profile—her slightly blurred rustic speech, her outgoing fondness for people, her managerial ability, and her courage—Cabell courted her staidly. When she once remarked that she had decided not to marry him because she was his senior by some four and a half years, he proposed to her out of protest. Despite what she knew about him from hearsay, she accepted him.[40] They were married on November 8, 1913.

III *Marriage and Fame*

Reformed atheists are often in demand for revival meetings and lay sermons in the best churches. Reformed Communists are popular as lecturers before Rotary and Kiwanis clubs. Reformed drunkards frequently become active in Alcoholics Anonymous. But reformed rakes are usually left to the tender mercies of the women who have circumscribed their promiscuity. So it was with Cabell and the wife whom he insisted on calling Priscilla Bradley and who contributed to the Brown Woman of *The Certain Hour,* to the Kathleen Kennaston of *The Cream of the Jest,* to Dame Lisa, Chloris, and Anaïtis of *Jurgen,* to Niafer and Freydis of *Figures of Earth,* to Maya of the Fair Breasts of *Something About Eve,* and to most of the more "real" women of his later fictions.[41]

Domesticity was anything but uninteresting. He and his newly acquired, large family lived at the Shepherd home, where he had his way about certain renovations.[42] From the name of this residence—"Dumbarton Grange"—many people who never saw it got the impression that it was some kind of palatial mansion amid spacious, richly verdured grounds. Carl Van Vechten was surprised to discover that it was "a mediocre farmhouse, furnished in the most nondescript manner, adjacent to railroad tracks and subject to the frequent noisy interruption of passing trains" with "no spreading oaks or mammoth elms" surrounding it but only "vegetation . . . meager and unimposing."[43] Gradually Cabell won the affection of his four normal stepchildren. The nurse of the pathetically stricken Isabelle—Negress Martha Cousins who was altogether unlike Louisa Nelson—kept calling Priscilla "Mrs. Shepherd," predicted dire consequences for this second marriage, and—to put it plainly—made no bones about hating Cabell's guts.[44]

The dire consequences did not develop. Instead, Cabell and Priscilla Bradley transformed each other.[45] They achieved an admirable union and maintained it with unswerving loyalty for thirty-five years. It was to afford them ever deeper satisfactions through weal and woe.

Cabell continued his work as a professional genealogist, first with the Virginia Chapter of the Sons of the Revolution and later with other historical societies in the State. From 1919 to 1926 he was editor for the Virginia War History Commission. From the publication of *The Rivet in Grandfather's Neck* by Robert M. McBride and Company the second year after his marriage, the "Biography of the Life of Manuel" grew apace. *The Rivet*, although dedicated to Priscilla Bradley, had been completed the year before he met her.

Through his genealogical industry Cabell enabled Priscilla to embark early in their marriage on the kind of social career she could not aspire to as the wife of a lumber merchant and as the daughter of a Charles City County farmer whose antecedents were not known too well in Richmond. Delving into these antecedents, Cabell discovered that she was descended from some of the oldest and best families of Virginia. He set forth her family tree with all its branches and foliage in *The Majors and Their Marriages* (1915),[46] his third privately printed genealogical volume.

Thus restored to the true splendor of her heritage, Priscilla became a leader in numerous select, patriotic organizations. She saw to it that her three daughters—Priscilla Shepherd, Grace Shepherd, and Virginia Shepherd—had the best educations and made desirable marriages. Supervising his wife's public activities —as well as her speech, hairdo, and jewelry—Cabell felt like a Pygmalion who had created an always gracious, highly energetic Galatea or Eliza, with a competence in practical matters that continued to astonish him daily.[47]

On August 25, 1915, she presented him with a son, Ballard Hartwell, to whom they grew more and more attached.[48] She also took Cabell on Sunday mornings to Episcopal services. With superb efficiency, she managed the farm, the servants, the automobile, the housekeeping, social engagements, and the all-important maintenance of his privacy for creative writing.[49]

After Isabelle Shepherd's death, Priscilla Shepherd's marriage, the departure of Emmett, Jr., to work in Texas, and the engagements of both Grace and Virginia Shepherd, Priscilla Bradley informed Cabell that "Dumbarton Grange" was much too large for them. So in 1925 they disposed of it and bought a suitable home in Richmond on Monument Avenue. They spent their summers at "Cayford Cottage," the retreat they had built at Mountain Lake, Virginia; there in a glass-enclosed, small porch-room Cabell wrote.[50]

As his fame—after the *Jurgen* imbroglio—spread far and wide and they began to form intimate friendships and to move socially in the world of well-known literary personages of the 1920's, Priscilla Bradley blossomed into a literary hostess, chaperone, and press-agent without peer. She was everywhere admired and respected, but she seldom read beyond the first few pages of her husband's books and never pretended to read any of the works of his newly acquired friends and acquaintances.[51]

Among the friends, Guy Holt—editor for McBride and later for the John Day Company—deserves special mention. He helped Cabell almost as much as Maxwell Perkins of Scribner's and Edward C. Aswell of Harper's later helped another southern writer, Thomas Wolfe. It was Holt who accepted *The Rivet* and *The Cream of the Jest*. Conversations with him led Cabell to write the prologue to the "Biography of the Life of Manuel," *Beyond Life*, in which he not only expounded his theory of romance and "dynamic illusions" but also defined the three attitudes—the chivalrous, the gallant, and the poetic—that the entire "Biography" seeks to dramatize.[52]

Inspired by a youthful editor so different from Henry Mills Alden, Cabell imagined what it would be like if his alter ego, the Devil, should kidnap the efficient Priscilla Bradley and if, in the effort to get her back, he might also recover his youthful body and yet keep the mature philosophic mind he now possessed and—miracle of miracles—re-encounter rejuvenated versions of some of the more memorable ladies he had known during those fled seasons at the Rockbridge Alum. The result was *Jurgen,* a profoundly personal fantasy—a prose saga of nostalgic libertinism such as no one had attempted since Byron wrote *Don Juan,* the great poetic saga on this theme. *Jurgen* was also as convincing a defense of monogamy as Homer's *Odyssey.*[53]

Censorship of an especially narrow and unintelligent type had long kept writers in both England and the United States from treating aspects of experience that Continental writers had felt free and even obligated to take into account in their best work ever since the trial and exoneration of Flaubert's *Madame Bovary.* This Anglo-American censorship followed the traditional Puritan practice of making the author's subject-matter, rather than his attitudes toward it, the final test of obscenity, lasciviousness, lewdness, and indecency.[54] It thus failed to discriminate between pornography and serious art. It took no reckoning of subtleties of moral implication; it was obtuse to what Cabell has termed "the urbanity of nuance."[55]

This censorship persecuted the Vizetellys in England for issuing even expurgated translations of Zola. Writers as distinguished as George Moore and Bernard Shaw had felt its fury. In the United States one of its self-appointed fomenters had been Anthony Comstock. Comstockery, affecting the taste and conscience of the wife of Frank Doubleday, led this publisher to withhold Dreiser's *Sister Carrie* from circulation after the first edition was printed and bound. The fear of Comstockery's legal power, wielded by the Western Society for the Prevention of Vice in Cincinnati and by John S. Sumner, executive secretary for the New York Society for the Suppression of Vice, forced the John Lane Company to withdraw Dreiser's *The "Genius."*[56] It was this same Sumner who, on January 14, 1920, armed with a warrant, appeared in McBride's offices, seized the plates and all copies of *Jurgen,* and summoned the corporation and its book department manager, Guy Holt, to answer next day in court a charge of violating Section 1141 of the Penal Code of the State of New York.[57]

Ironically enough, Carl Van Vechten, who was soon to become one of Cabell's closest friends, may have inadvertently set in motion the train of circumstances that culminated in Sumner's raid. When *Jurgen* was already in its third edition and was receiving reviews praising its literary merits, the enthusiastic Van Vechten babbled too much about its improprieties to a theatrical press agent, Walter J. Kingsley,[58] who presently wrote a letter to the New York *Tribune* protesting that Cabell was getting away with murder. This letter provoked others; a veritable controversy was under way, one issue being how to read *Jurgen* to ferret out all the smut. Someone, disturbed by this trend toward prurience, mailed Sumner a clipping of Kingsley's letter. Sumner got a copy of *Jurgen;* concluded it was a stew laced with lubricities such as the obviously phallic symbolism of the hero's lance, staff, and sword; and moved quickly to protect public morals.

The mob spirit was striking at Cabell a third time. Little wonder that he was to tell those asking about the pronunciation of his surname that it rhymed with rabble![59] This time he fought back more vigorously than ever before. Postponements of trial, after the initial hearing, gave the publishers and their attorneys over two and a half years to prepare their defense and to circulate petitions protesting the censorship. Cabell kept closely in touch with these efforts, revised several of his earlier books for reissue, and wrote *Figures of Earth*—major companion romance to *Jurgen*—as well as *Taboo,* a savage satire on Sumner and his supporters.

Cabell enjoyed the satisfaction of having *Jurgen* published in a fine English edition. Then the trial began on October 16, 1922; on October 19, Judge Charles C. Nott, of the New York Court of General Sessions, directed the jury to bring in a verdict of acquittal. McBride was soon issuing *Jurgen* at somewhat the same rate that years later Random House was to issue Joyce's *Ulysses;* Putnam's Sons, Nabokov's *Lolita;* and the Grove Press, Lawrence's *Lady Chatterley's Lover* and Miller's *Tropic of Cancer.*

The presence of Ellen Glasgow, and now the presence of the author of *Beyond Life* and *Jurgen,* focused the nation's attention on Richmond as a literary center in the early 1920's. What clinched its pre-eminence, for a while at least, was the publication there of *The Reviewer* between February, 1921, and October, 1924. First planned during the initial excitement over the suppression of *Jurgen,* this unusual "little magazine," the joint enterprise of four of the city's young literati—Emily Clark, Margaret Waller Freeman, Mary Dallas Street, and Hunter Stagg—published an astonishing number of new—as well as established—American and British writers and brought many of them to town as visitors. Cabell advised the editors at their meetings, which took the form of parties; he also guest-edited *The Reviewer* single-handed for October, November, and December, 1921, and was throughout its existence a most willing contributor.[60]

From 1917 to 1929, indeed, Cabell was functioning in a kind of axial relationship with his admirers, not only in Richmond, but in many other places. In Chicago, Burton Rascoe early promoted a Cabell boom and controversy.[61] In Baltimore, H. L. Mencken championed—with occasional reservations—almost every book Cabell published. In Atlanta, Frances Newman put him into *The Hard-Boiled Virgin* as Charles Carrington. In West Chester, Pennsylvania, Joseph Hergesheimer cherished him as one of the world's great writers.[62] In New York, Carl Van Vechten idolized him even more than he did Ronald Firbank, while Benjamin DeCasseres hailed him as a new Prometheus.[63] John Macy, Sinclair Lewis, and Hugh Walpole were among his more roving intimates.[64]

In 1927 McBride began the publication of the eighteen-volume, green-and-gold Storisende Edition of *The Works of James Branch Cabell* which sold at ten dollars a volume. Fiction displaying the Cabellian touch began to appear with increasing frequency: Lorine Pruette's *Saint in Ivory* (1927), Elmer Davis' *Giant Killer* and Djuna Barnes's *Ryder* (both 1928), and Louis Kronenberger's *The Grand Manner* (1929).[65] Then broke the Great Depression, and the Cabell-centered 1920's dissolved into thin air, along with the forlorn "sophisticated" spirits of Frances Newman, Elinor Wylie, and Donn Byrne.[66]

IV *Last Decades*

Although Cabell's curiosity about the human comedy remained as alive as ever, the America of the Depression and New Deal years, of World War II, and of the atomic age and the Cold War became increasingly offensive to his sense of dignity and order. The depredations of time were manifesting themselves also in his and Priscilla's bodies as well as in the body politic.

Resolute to carry the skeptical, critical spirit of the 1920's into the planned, nostrum-hungry climate of the early New Deal, Cabell joined George Jean Nathan, Ernest Boyd, Theodore Dreiser, Eugene O'Neill, and Sherwood Anderson, who eventually was added to the group, in editing *The American Spec-*

tator between 1932 and 1935. The venture stimulated Cabell's interest in essay writing but it made only a passing and superficial impact on current opinion, literary or otherwise.

After January 14, 1935, Cabell suffered repeated attacks of pneumonia that necessitated frequent removals to St. Augustine, Florida. Toward midsummer of 1936, Priscilla Bradley developed arthritis that grew steadily worse, called for regular hospital treatments, and forced the abandonment of "Cayford Cottage" because of its difficult terrain. Immediately the Cabells built the new summer cottage "Poynton Lodge" in the level lowlands of Northumberland County, Virginia.[67]

The books Cabell continued to write—at first under the name of Branch Cabell and then under his full name again—reflected considerable disillusionment with the readers who had once made a cult of his work for the wrong reasons, harassed his leisure with letters and other communications, and sought shamelessly to invade his privacy.[68] The dream of Poictesme turned into the mock-Freudian "nightmare" of *Smirt, Smith,* and *Smire.* In the last two of these fantasies, Smirt, the sardonically christened Virginia novelist, showed he was still smitten with myth and able to express his ire with a smile, as one persona faded into the next. Experiment with comedy went merrily on in *The King Was in His Counting House, Hamlet Had an Uncle, The First Gentleman of America, There Were Two Pirates,* and *The Devil's Own Dear Son.* Cabell's own past and the legendry and history of both Virginia and Florida came more and more to absorb his attention.

Friendships with Stephen Vincent Benét, A. J. Hanna—professor of history at Rollins College, Florida—and Marjorie Kinnan Rawlings replaced some of his earlier attachments.[69] Although he did not forsake McBride entirely, he turned to other publishers—particularly to Farrar and Rinehart and later to Farrar and Straus, as well as Doubleday, Doran and Company, and the University of Florida Press.

After twelve years of courageous suffering as an arthritic, Priscilla Bradley had heart failure in St. Augustine the evening of March 25, 1949; she died after four drugged and tortured days in the Flagler Hospital, and was buried on All Fools' Day. Her long decline and terrible passing left Cabell with a feeling of irreparable loss, as well as an embittered, shaken faith in the notions of justice held by the Episcopalian God they both had worshiped.[70]

This faith was soon to be partially restored, however, through the aid of Ballard, who suggested that Margaret Waller Freeman would make a good stepmother. Cabell had always been vividly aware of her since those perished golden days on *The Reviewer*. Though she was young enough to be his daughter, Cabell courted her. They were married on June 15, 1950. Thus, with "another fearless woman," the time-battered romancer completed his education serenely[71] before Grandfather Death struck him down with a cerebral hemorrhage on May 5, 1958, at the age of seventy-nine.

CHAPTER 2

Approaches to the "Biography of the Life of Manuel"

I *Schema*

CABELL insisted that the eighteen volumes of the Storisende Edition of his *Works* should be regarded as a single book, with its prologue, epilogue, chapters, appendices, and commentary. He chose the covering label "Biography of the Life of Manuel" only after weighing it carefully against "Biography of Manuel" and "The Life of Manuel." He rejected the latter two as equally inaccurate, for the series was concerned not only with the account of Manuel's career but also with the histories of various of his descendants for seven generations.

One line of his descendants started with Alianora in England. The earlier main line began with Niafer in Poictesme—imaginary medieval realm named after the actual provinces of Poictiers and Angoulêsme.[1] A third line were descendants in a more figurative sense, the offspring of eleven images that Manuel and Freydis "informed with fire from Audela and set to live as abnormal men among normal mankind."[2]

"Biography of the Life of Manuel," then, although an awkward and at first glance tautological label, is the only precise one. "Life" stands for the stream of vital energy in the most comprehensive sense, as entering into and passed on by Manuel and as modified by other "life," particularly that of Jurgen—Manuel's mighty opposite.[3]

Beyond Life, as prologue, provides "the vital and aesthetic theories thereafter builded on," and it indicates "the forces to which my protagonist later reacts and the three codes by which, at one or another time, he is swayed."[4] "Then in *Figures of*

Earth and *The Silver Stallion* is comprised the entire career of Manuel, as he appeared in the eyes of those who knew him best in life, and, also, as he appeared in the eyes of those same persons, and of yet other persons, after his passing out of life."[5] The chivalric code or chivalrous attitude, triumphing over the poetic, takes shape in Manuel—at least as some saw him—and becomes a kind of religion in his legend. Next *Domnei* treats one tenet of this code—woman-worship.

In the same volume with *Domnei* in the Storisende Edition appears *The Music from Behind the Moon*. This *nouvelle* about Madoc's quest of the witch-woman Ettarre treats woman-worship as transmuted by the poetic attitude. Relegated to the Storisende Edition's last volume are two other *nouvelles* that have to do with Ettarre—*The Way of Ecben,* wherein she is loved by an exemplar of chivalry; and *The White Robe,* wherein her adorer is an exponent of gallantry. Many years after the publication of the Storisende Edition, Cabell reissued these three *nouvelles* in a slender volume entitled *The Witch-Woman,* indicating that they should be read together as companion pieces to *Domnei.* A sequel to *Domnei* is *Chivalry,* short stories about characters committed to another chivalrous tenet—"final responsibility to a divine Father"—but not always living up to this finality.[6]

The code or attitude of gallantry, in triumphant collusion and conflict with the poetic attitude, is next displayed in *Jurgen.* All three attitudes—the chivalrous, the gallant, and the poetic—occur in the short stories of *The Line of Love. The High Place* and the short stories of *Gallantry* "return to yet clearer examples of the gallant attitude, and appraise it, severally, in its failure and in its relative success."[7] *Something About Eve* and the stories of *The Certain Hour,* ranging forward toward modern times, "illustrate the failure, and . . . the success, of the poet's attitude toward life."[8]

The next four major fictions of the "Biography" are set in a world more closely identifiable with the world of Cabell's youth and bachelor years. *The Cords of Vanity* is "a portrait of the gallant person in modern conditions."[9] It has two appendices—a collection of poems, *From the Hidden Way,* and a play, *The Jewel Merchants.* The poems—and to some extent the play—are designed to reveal further facets of this gallant person's psyche, just as "The Revolutionist's Handbook" helps one to understand John Tanner in Shaw's *Man and Superman*. *The Rivet in Grandfather's Neck* portrays a modern chivalrous person. "Then, with *The Eagle's Shadow* and *The Cream of the Jest*, the story of the Biography is rounded off, just as the long story began, with yet another two-volume comedy, presenting the poet in modern conditions,—and presenting, also, the manner of this Felix Kennaston's return into Poictesme, whereby the life of Manuel ends its seven long centuries of journeying at the point of its outset."[10]

Appropriately bound up with *The Cream of the Jest* is *The Lineage of Lichfield*, a genealogy of many of the "Biography's" characters. *Straws and Prayer-Books*, the epilogue, complementing *Beyond Life*, "explains . . . why the Biography was written."[11] *Townsend of Lichfield*, the final volume, takes care of divers odds and ends from the "Biography's" workshop, so to speak.

"Yes: to me," says Cabell, "the Biography appears a tolerably complete and symmetrical affair, an affair of three main themes regarded each from a quartet of varying standpoints."[12] By this, he apparently means that each of the three attitudes is treated in its older and its modern forms and in its successful as well as failing embodiments. Later, in *Some of Us*, he admits to drawbacks. One is that "this scheme . . . tends over strongly to suggest an exercise in arithmetic rather than in aesthetics." Another is that "To demand of your readers that they labor through no modest Iliad-length of some 16,000 hexameters, but through eighteen extensive volumes, in order to find out just what the writer may be driving at, is to ignore a great deal more widely than did Homer's blindness the firm limits of human nature."[13]

II *A Fourth Dimension of Regionalism*

"Regionalism" as a sociological term connotes the opposite of "sectionalism." The sectionalist is a narrow-minded patriot, exalting the virtues and interests of his part of the country at the expense of the nation as a whole, but the regionalist keeps the whole nation in mind and conceives of its welfare as dependent upon the distinctive contributions of its parts. He is a critical humanist seeking to discover his region's powers and weaknesses, so that its contribution can be a sound one.

Regionalism as a literary term is less clear. It is sometimes

used merely as a synonym for a writer's concern with "local color."
Again, it may imply his deeper quest for the forces at work in
a given locale rather than his preoccupation with the surface pic-
turesqueness of its people, customs, or settings. The literary regionalist who is something more than a local colorist may also
be considered a kind of humanistic critic; he interprets his part
of the country to readers elsewhere so as to promote sympathy
and understanding.

After the Civil War, literary regionalism of this type began
to serve the ends of sociological regionalism, perhaps most often
unconsciously. The writer dedicated to place set about instinc-
tively implementing Lincoln's injunction to "bind up the nation's
wounds."[14] He broke down sectional prejudices by the processes
of vicarious experience. The southern regionalist, such as Thomas
Nelson Page, made northern and western readers pity and love
the proud South in her acceptance of defeat. The northern regionalist, such as Sarah Orne Jewett or Mary Wilkins Freeman, stirred
southern and western readers to understand the conflict between
duty and pleasure in the inheritors of puritanism, or the quaint
persistence of an old identification with the will of God in
instances of their domestic tenderness and stubbornness. The
western regionalist, such as Bret Harte, impressed on his eastern audience, both in the North and in the South, the presence
of hearts of gold in the roughest characters of frontier towns.[15]
There were even regionalists on the move, such as Constance
Fenimore Woolson and Opie Read.[16]

Since the 1870's three main modes of literary regionalism have
succeeded each other in the United States—the sentimental, the
realistic, and the symbolic. The sentimentalist has looked nos-
talgically at his region's remote or recent past and distorted
it somewhat for the purpose of evoking sympathy. The realist,
who has assumed the role of the objective social historian, has
stripped away emotional veils and their myths and stereotypes
from the region's past and present so as to bring into plain view
hard facts and actual forces. The symbolist, who has transmuted
the region's past-present continuum into a microcosm of the
human scene, has substituted new myths for old and has found
universal significance in minutely observed provincial particulars. In southern regional fiction one can observe this threefold
development clearly as one moves from Mary Noailles Murfree to
Ellen Glasgow to William Faulkner.

Cabell's stories of modern Virginia betray the presence of both the sentimental and realistic regionalist. Certainly also he makes use of symbols and myths in them as well as in his fictions about more imaginary places. But when the "Biography" is viewed as a whole, its regionalism emerges as of a quite different mode from that associated with Miss Murfree's Great Smoky Mountains stories, or Ellen Glasgow's novels of commonwealth, country, and city,[17] or Faulkner's Yoknapatawpha County cycle. For Cabell is presenting a spiritual Prose Edda of Virginia that dramatizes its traditional values directly, relates them to their remote English and Continental origins, and shows what has happened to them in modern adumbrations. He is an allegorical rather than a sentimental, realistic, or symbolic regionalist.

Allegory is astringent to sentimentalism by virtue of the subordination of emotions to ideas or concepts. Allegory presents somewhat-larger-than-life characters whose powers transcend the meager abilities and limitations of characters in realistic fiction. Allegory differs from symbolism in the same way that the deductive method differs from the inductive, to which it is so closely connected. The allegorist presents personified abstractions whose stories are fertile in their applications to many specific aspects of human life, while the symbolist treats such specific aspects so as to suggest spires or levels of more general meaning.[18]

The allegorical regionalist can do more than merely personify and dramatize the values characteristic of his culture. He can be normative as well as retrospectively interpretive. In other words, he can give life to the values signally neglected by his culture and thus serve as its constructively critical iconoclast. This aspect of his allegory may prove prophetic and redemptive.[19]

The chivalrous, gallant, and poetic *dramatis personae* of the "Biography" may be approached in the light of these several generalizations about allegorical regionalism. To do so, it is convenient to have before one Cabell's most succinct definition of his three attitudes: "The descendants of Manuel have at various times very variously viewed life as a testing; as a toy; and as raw material. They have variously sought during their existence upon earth to become—even by the one true test, of their private thoughts while lying awake at night—admirable; or to enjoy life; or to create something more durable than life."[20]

To view life as a testing, to seek to become admirable—these impulses of chivalry, coming down to Virginia and the South from the Middle Ages and the English Renaissance, inspired military and political careers. The general and the statesman were the ideal men. At its best this tradition cherished the notion that Cabell has called "vicarship"—that its ideal men were mundane representatives of their Christian God. And at its best this tradition also cherished the notion that Cabell has called "domnei"—that good, true, and beautiful women were to be reverenced as the secondary representatives of omnipotence.[21] But such a tradition and such values were difficult for men to keep living up to. Puritanism—with its overemphasis on piety—and Philistinism—with its overemphasis on common sense, practicality, and conformity—might easily corrupt a code so exalted in its views and aims, so inclined to make a fetish of the will, and so definitely oriented toward success in the domain of public action.

To view life as a toy, to seek to enjoy life—these impulses of gallantry, coming down to Virginia and the South from the Caroline cavaliers, the Restoration, and the eighteenth century— were a kind of reaction against the high-mindedness of chivalry and the corruption of its values by New England Puritanism and Yankee Philistinism. The rationale of gallantry was libertine and skeptical. The practice of gallantry led to hedonism in all its forms. The attention the gallant paid women was more exploratory than reverential. The faculty he prized above all others was the intelligence rather than the will—and he might play with ideas as well as with morals. A social life where gracious manners were prized above strict morals was gallantry's supreme cultural achievement in the English and Continental past, and in Virginia and other parts of the South. But such an achievement was also subject to corruption. Compromise, conformity, hypocrisy, mountebankery, Philistinism, and the stultification of the creative urge might creep in, as Cabell's John Charteris demonstrates in *Beyond Life* by reviewing the careers of Congreve and Sheridan. At the springs of Virginia and among his friends and acquaintances of the 1920's, Cabell himself found abundant evidence of such disquieting outcomes in gallantry's gay worlds.

To view life as raw material, to seek to create something more durable than life—these impulses of the poet or artist, coming down to Virginia and the South in its Hellenic, medieval, Renaissance, and romantic legacies—did not operate importantly in the traditional chivalric and gallant culture. The poetic impulses were, of course, there from the start; but they could not cope effectively with the attractions of military, political, and other practical professional careers nor with the distractions of polite society. The poet might celebrate chivalry and gallantry as "dynamic illusions" behind his "beautiful happenings," but his own economy of living was at war with divine and social ordinances, with the limiting pressures of reality, with common sense and piety and death.

In *Beyond Life,* Cabell's John Charteris holds up Marlowe and Villon, poets living in periods when chivalrous deeds were often done and gallant frivolities were coming into vogue, as exponents of this poetic economy. In *Straws and Prayer-Books,* dismissing John Charteris, Cabell in his own person outlines the poet's playing with common sense and piety and death in an anchoritic self-diversion, to perpetuate his own ideas and personality. To flout common sense, he points out, Donn Byrne recreated Marco Polo. To the scandal of piety, Charles de Coster retraced Tyll Eulenspiegel's roguish folk adventuring. To mock at death, Anatole France set the Abbé Jérôme Coignard about his escapades and religious meditations. For self-diversion but also for self-perpetuation, Joseph Hergesheimer wrote for long years without recognition; and George Moore finally produced, after patient revision of his earlier publishings, the fine Carra Edition of them—both writers, in these respects, being comparable to Cabell himself. The poet's guiding faculty—as Cabell conceives him—is neither the will nor the intelligence, although he must exercise both in full measure. Rather the poet is dominated by the imagination—Coleridge's "esemplastic power," Santayana's custodian of the realm of essence, Wallace Stevens' unique, causal reality.[22]

By devoting so much of the "Biography" to exponents of the poetic attitude and by showing traces of this attitude both in his chivalrous and gallant characters, Cabell made his allegorical regionalism normative, constructively critical, iconoclastic, prophetic, and redemptive. He condemned the Virginia that turned Poe into an Ishmael; and he helped blaze the way for the many able creative spirits of the contemporary "Southern Renascence," even though most of them perhaps regard his conception of the poet as too elementary in its essentials and too decadent in its elaboration.

III   *"As If" Versus "Nothing But"*

The intellectual climate from the 1890's to the end of the 1920's can best be understood as a many-sided conflict. Two forms of philosophical naturalism confronted each other, and one may be described as reductive. Deriving authority from the biological and natural sciences, it sought to discredit all forms of traditional realism and idealism as resting on supernaturalistic fallacies. God was *nothing but* force and light in the cosmos; the soul was *nothing but* the consciousness of existence. Consciousness itself and all its faculties—the intuition, the will, the reason, the imagination, and the memory—were *nothing but* the organism's hereditarily determined responses to stimuli from its environment. Order and purpose in the universe and society were *nothing but* mechanical equilibrium and repetition produced by certain regularities in the motion of objects in space, by the workings of blind chance or circumstance in time, and by the processes of adaptation and habit on the part of individuals and groups.

The least extreme alternative to this militantly materialistic way of thought, with its dogmatic manipulation of *nothing but,* was constructive naturalism. The premise herein was the emergence of subtler dichotomies in the long evolutionary process. The universals and spiritual entities postulated by traditional realists and idealists would in the course of time come to have—naturally and inevitably, without divine fiat or inspired human intervention—a valid existence, an independent ontological status.

Peripheral to these forms of naturalism, but not diametrically opposed to either, were various pragmatisms,[23] most of which had in common the assumption that truth could be established only by a radically empirical procedure. Any hypothesis in the physical and biological sciences that "worked" toward clearer ordering of the facts from which it was derived and that at the same time "checked" with the already established body of hypotheses in its area of investigation was tentatively, relatively, or provisionally a "truth." Any hypothesis in the social sciences—which included such normative fields of philosophy as ethics and aesthetics—was also "true" if it "worked" and "checked" in the same way. By the pragmatic tests, many of the absolutes of traditional realism and idealism—and of religion and theology—were salvageable as usable "fictions" in a scientific age.

Traditional realism, harking back to Aristotle, Aquinas, and Avicenna, did not surrender to the naturalisms and pragmatisms thus described. Although drawn to the position of the constructive naturalist, the modern philosophical realist defended his belief in universals, in the dualism of the *res interna* and the *res externa,* and in reason as the best way to knowledge —the ultimate criterion of truth—by other arguments than the appeal to the evolutionary process. He sometimes fell into the fallacy, however, of attaching to the term "reason" the same uncritically eulogistic implications that he charged some of his opponents attached to such terms as "life," "experience," "reality," or "imagination."[24]

Idealism held its ground against naturalism and pragmatism in their various forms and, although sympathetic with the revival of traditional realism, distrusted not only its excessive reliance on the reason but also the compromises and mediations to which this reliance usually led. The idealist—sometimes calling himself a personalist—insisted on the primacy of consciousness or spirit and its essences or symbols. Truth existed only in these. In purer mood, the idealist held that the realm of matter seemingly reported by the senses was actually a projection through them from the human imagination functioning under the intuitional inspiration of a supernaturalistic deity. To mold such a world to one's thinking and one's desire by heroic action was like carrying iconic coals to an illusory Newcastle.

As these various "isms" competed for attention and priority in the intellectual climate, libertine skepticism—a mode of thinking Hellenic in origin but Renaissance and eighteenth-century in transmission—might serve either of two compulsions. Thus it tended to become equivocal, ambiguous, paradoxical, ironical, oxymoronic, and schizophrenic. Either it began by doubting the absolutes of idealism and thence—after dallying with realism's less noble compromises—staggered in the direction of the various pragmatisms and the two naturalisms—and perhaps ultimately fell into the gutters of cynicism and negation; or its first step was to question the material reality postulated by science. When skepticism so behaved, it moved easily to constructive naturalism or to realism's more noble mediations and thence to pragmatic idealism. It could end—and often did—in religious affirmation. The most provocative and tenable of these positions in an age of science was the mixed one of pragmatic idealism—

sometimes referred to as *bovarysme*—which insisted that man might make some of his dreams come true by acting as if they all would.[25] This *as if* philosophy was an effective counterblast to the *nothing but* dogmatism of the reductive naturalist. For to the riddle of what has been termed "the place of value in a world of facts" it offered a solution resolutely frivolous—cockily humane.[26]

This sketch of philosophical positions in conflict from the 1890's to the end of the 1920's is, of course, drastically—and in some respects absurdly—oversimplified, but it will have to serve the purpose of viewing Cabell as something more than an allegorical regionalist. Approached in terms of the "isms" here briefly defined, the "Biography of the Life of Manuel" is a richly expressive, bewilderingly ambivalent, creative response to a most complex transitional period in the history of Western thought. During the "Biography's" long making, Cabell—whose basic orientation as an amateur or "literary" thinker was that of libertine skepticism—ran virtually the whole gamut of ideas being mulled over by professional naturalists, pragmatists, realists, and idealists.

Partly with reference to these ideas and their possible combinations, Cabell conceived and set moving his chivalrous, gallant, and poetic characters. Not always sure of the precise position where his skepticism was most at home, he presented his prologue and epilogue as a give-and-take between different spokesmen. In *Beyond Life*, Cabell himself appears as more interested in purely literary than in philosophical issues. The task of giving "romance" and "realism" their larger meanings falls to John Charteris. In *Straws and Prayer-Books*, the sophisticated Cabell—the author of *Jurgen*—at first re-engages Charteris; then takes over the argument as his own monologue; interrupts this monologue with remembered conversations and with parables—"The Thin Queen of Elfhame" and "The Delta of Radegonde"; and in the last chapter finds himself confronted by the more naïve Cabell who wrote *The Eagle's Shadow*. In most of the fictions—from Poictesme to Lichfield—the dialogue as well as the narration constantly presents ideas, and sometimes at the expense of the illusion of reality or supra-reality that the romancer is endeavoring to create and maintain.

As John Charteris talks the night away in *Beyond Life*, he is anything but consistent; he veers now in one of the directions taken by the modern skeptic and again in the other. Cabell, who aptly describes him as "Well-primed, if not exactly tipsy, with the home-brew of his own verbosity," is inclined to forgive him on the following thoroughly skeptical ground: "All human ideas . . . should be valued only as the playthings with which one purchases diversion. One plays with them during the night-season of a not yet ended Walburga's Eve upon which almost anything is rather more than likely to happen."[27]

In *Quiet, Please* Cabell states that the main drift of Charteris' "comments upon love, chivalry, patriotism, gallantry, virtue, creative literature, religion and yet other amenities of our existence" is that they are "dynamic illusions" or "highflown fictions as to human living which make human living endurable, and indeed, to the best of my experience, a most interesting and fervent, if inconsequent, performance."[28] This later summary has overtones that suggest Cabell had intended Charteris to be a sly, reductive naturalist showing that the loftiest enterprises and goals of the race are *nothing but* its occupational therapies and aphrodisiacs which prevent crack-up and promote potency.

But as one returns to *Beyond Life* and follows Charteris to the end, one finds that the demiurgic spirit of romance contriving these "dynamic illusions" has a real existence and an ultimately benign purpose that man fulfills. "The things of which romance assures him," says Charteris, "are very far from true: yet it is solely by believing himself a creature but little lower than the cherubim that man has by interminable small degrees become, upon the whole, distinctly superior to the chimpanzee."[29] "We are being made into something quite unpredictable, I imagine: and we are sustained, through the purging and the smelting, by an instinctive knowledge that we are being made into something better. . . . it is this will that stirs in us to have the creatures of earth and the affairs of earth, not as they are, but 'as they ought to be,' which we call romance. But when we note how visibly it sways all life we perceive that we are talking about God."[30] Charteris has moved quickly to points smacking of both constructive naturalism and pragmatic idealism and has concluded on a note of religious affirmation. In *Straws and Prayer-Books*, Cabell in his own person strikes out in behalf of the pragmatist and the idealist when he calls attention to the fictional or mythic aspects of money and mathematics. One is the basis of practical life, the other of science; yet each is controlled by the same romancing that enters into poetry and religion.

The kind of idealism that goes hand in hand with religion, that fosters religious commitments, revivals, and institutions— sometimes unwittingly—dominates Cabell's chivalrous characters at their best. The toploftiness of their dreams, however, makes them vulnerable to ultimate disillusion and defeat, life being the unfinished, imperfect process that it is. As for Cabell's gallant characters, their skepticism reacts constantly to chivalrous heights and rigidities. In the pursuit of intellectual and physical pleasures, they court realistic, pragmatic, naturalistic perspectives. Content to compromise with a world that they think they had no share in making and can never change, they pride themselves on being safe from ultimate disillusionments and catastrophic defeats; but, none the less, time holds for them discomforting surprises.

The Cabellian poets are the genuine pragmatic idealists. If they can stick to their tasks of giving ever finer shape to their dreams, they can thwart time and build for themselves and others a life beyond life. Shirking the task work that their dreams impose and yielding to the pressure of reality in their age and place, they too become time's victims.

These Cabellian type-characters, recurring with variations from book to book of the "Biography," play off the *as if* against the *nothing but* in a sustained dramatic dialectic.

IV *The Comedic Metaphor Expanded*

The Shakespearean comedy of gayety, the Jonsonian comedy of humors, the Restoration comedy of manners, and the Shavian comedy of ideas—these were the great comic stage traditions in English literature that affected Cabell's thinking as he sought to expand into full-length romances and shorter tales the comedic metaphor suggested by his genealogical research. Undoubtedly, also, through his Greek and French studies he was well acquainted with Aristophanes' comedy of myths and with Molière's comedy of common sense.

So far as prose fiction was concerned, he had ample warrant, precedent, and current competition for the achievement in narrative of effects associated with one or more of these stage traditions. Fielding, Smollett, Jane Austen, Dickens, and Thackeray had built the comedy of humors and of manners into the English novel. George Meredith related the comedy of gayety and the comedy of common sense in his theory of the comic spirit and in his greatest novel, *The Egoist: A Comedy in Narrative,* as well as in several of its predecessors and successors. Finally, Cabell's contemporary, Maurice Hewlett—who had begun as a writer of romances and tales concerned with aspects of the chivalrous and gallant past—turned Meredithian in his trilogy *Open Country: A Comedy with a Sting* (1909), *Halfway House: A Comedy of Degrees* (1908), and *Rest Harrow: A Comedy of Resolution* (1910). Cabell's mixed admiration and contempt for Hewlett— the contempt partly motivated by Hewlett's derogation of Cabell as a medieval romancer—is one of the curious items in Cabell's complex relations to the English literature of his time.[31]

In the "Biography" most of the short stories and *nouvelles* can be classified as comic or tragi-comic. After the precedent of Meredith's *The Egoist,* all the longer fictions treating the three attitudes carry subtitles beginning with "A Comedy." Listing those about the chivalrous attitude in the order in which they should be read, one has *Figures of Earth: A Comedy of Appearances; The Silver Stallion: A Comedy of Redemption; Domnei: A Comedy of Woman-Worship;* and *The Rivet in Grandfather's Neck: A Comedy of Limitations.* Similarly, for the gallant attitude, one has *Jurgen: A Comedy of Justice; The High Place: A Comedy of Disenchantment;* and *The Cords of Vanity: A Comedy of Shirking.* Finally, for the poetic attitude, there are *Something About Eve: A Comedy of Fig-Leaves; The Eagle's Shadow: A Comedy of Purse-Strings;* and *The Cream of the Jest: A Comedy of Evasion.* These subtitles, as in the case of both Meredith and Hewlett, reveal a good deal about the author's intentions. They certainly justify approaching the "Biography" as "a comic epic in prose"—to borrow Fielding's definition of the novel—or as an elaborate experiment to capture the comic spirit in a romance cycle.

So approached, the "Biography" is seen to depart in one important respect from the comic tradition of the English novel. Although this tradition, from Fielding to Hewlett, is primarily social, the "Biography"—while including social comedy in its stories of the eighteenth century and of modern Virginia—achieves what may better be termed "cosmic comedy" because it puts its protagonist—the life of Manuel—against the universe and the gods. One of Cabell's most fervent admirers, Benjamin DeCasseres, argues in "The Comic View"—an essay in his Nietzschean-like

Chameleon—that comedy can be more truly cosmic than tragedy but that, to achieve this Olympian perspective, the comic artist has to traverse the shadowed valley of negations and to survive trysts with its demons.[32] Cabell's comedy, with its final serene detachment after much trafficking in cynicism, answers to such a description.

Another point yielded by concentration on the "Biography" as comedy is that there is perhaps more of Aristophanes and Shaw in it than of Jonson, Molière, Etherege, Wycherley, and Congreve. It is—at its best—a comedy of attitudes rather than a comedy of humors or manners. And the main attitudes—the chivalrous, the gallant, and the poetic—are linked to both myths and ideas in the Aristophanic and Shavian sense. Although the terms "comedy of myths" and "comedy of ideas" have been used to differentiate the work of Aristophanes and Shaw, the differentiation is merely one of emphasis. Such a mythological comedy as Aristophanes' *The Birds* is rich in ideas; such a philosophical comedy as Shaw's *Man and Superman* exploits myths. Like Aristophanes, Cabell erects his Cloud-Cuckoo-Land against Olympus and satirizes aspects of democracy. Like Shaw, Cabell takes his Don Juans to hell and his other supermen to comparably myth-infested places, involves them with avatars of the witch-woman, and, in the end, reveals their journeys and ensnarements as the design of a Life-Force.

A third point that becomes clear when one approaches the "Biography" as comedy is that it possesses certain Shakespearean characteristics. One student of Elinor Wylie has demonstrated that she had a Shelley obsession.[33] It can also be demonstrated—although this relatively short book is scarcely the place for it—that Cabell had a Shakespeare obsession, if one considers his many references to the plays, his portrayal of Shakespeare as one of his poetic protagonists in *The Certain Hour*, and his use of Falstaff in *The Line of Love* and *Ladies and Gentlemen*, of Prospero in *These Restless Heads*, and of Hamlet in *Ladies and Gentlemen* and *Hamlet Had an Uncle*.

The presence of Shakespeare in the "Biography" is first apparent in the quality of its prevailing laughter. Found in abundance is the laughter that arises from a sense of superiority. This is the type that predominates in satire, is of the mind, and is directed at—rather than oriented with—certain of the *dramatis personae*. Often it merely glances at more general instances of vice and

JAMES BRANCH CABELL

folly and dullness—human, divine, or demonic. Sometimes, too, occurs another type of laughter *at*—the sort that is a reaction to the grosser incongruities. It is the laughter that one associates with farce; it is of the belly more than of the mind. Both these kinds of laughter are in Shakespeare's comedies, but neither is his hallmark. The truly Shakespearean laughter is that of gayety. This laughter *with* certain of the *dramatis personae* is stirred by their artfully blended wit and emotion and by their often miraculously managed triumphs over circumstance, and it proceeds from the spectators' contagiously affected hearts and minds, responding in unison. This kind of laughter is perhaps most pervasive in the "Biography" when the chivalrous, the gallant, and the poetic attain their dreams; or, when failing to attain them—or finding them, when attained, not worth all the effort—they contemplate the outcome with the appropriate emotions and take their exits with the right gestures.

The comedy of the "Biography" is also Shakespearean in a deeper, a subtler, a more inverted way. One of the major effects in the world of *Hamlet, Othello, King Lear,* and *Macbeth*—and to some extent in *Richard II, Romeo and Juliet, Julius Caesar, Troilus and Cressida, Antony and Cleopatra, Timon of Athens,* and *Coriolanus*—is "tragic waste," as A. C. Bradley has pointed out. He thus describes this "waste," which he calls "the centre" or "central feeling" of Shakespeare's tragedies:

> We seem to have before us a type of the mystery of the whole world, the tragic fact which extends far beyond the limits of tragedy. Everywhere, from the crushed rocks beneath our feet to the soul of man, we see power, intelligence, life and glory, which astound us and seem to call for our worship. And everywhere we see them perishing, devouring one another and destroying themselves, often with dreadful pain, as though they came into being for no other end. Tragedy is the typical form of this mystery, because that greatness of soul which it exhibits oppressed, conflicting and destroyed, is the highest existence in our view. It forces the mystery upon us, and it makes us realise so vividly the worth of that which is wasted that we cannot possibly seek comfort in the reflection that all is vanity.[34]

Cabell, in expanding the comedic metaphor suggested by his genealogical research, achieved in the "Biography" what can best be called "comic waste," an impression that is an analogue to Shakespeare's "tragic waste."

Over and yet over again the play of aspiration, quest, falling short, or attainment with disillusion, is enacted. The puppets and their wardrobes and props go regularly to the scrap-heap. But the play goes on, an eternally recurrent performance, a kind of perpetual peekaboo epiphany. Here, in "this unending captaincy of a forlorn hope, in this futile and obstinate romanticism of life's vaudeville"—as Cabell puts it in *The Lineage of Lichfield*[35]—is another mighty mystery. Cabellian comedy—to repeat from Bradley—"is the typical form of this mystery. . . . It forces the mystery upon us, and it makes us realize so vividly the worth of that which is wasted that we cannot possibly seek comfort in the reflection that all is vanity." Rather one must say with Cabell's John Charteris in *Beyond Life:* ". . . vanity is all. For man alone of animals plays the ape to his dreams."[36]

V *The Novel Flouted*

To enable one to talk more intelligently about prose fiction and to define the complexity and freedom of its workings, Northrop Frye in his *Anatomy of Criticism* has proposed that one no longer center on the novel—as the Ptolemaic astronomy centered on the earth—but relegate it to its real or proper orbit in the system of fiction—as the Copernican astronomy placed the earth between Mars and Venus.[37] He would restrict the term "novel" to extended prose narrative portraying typical or representative, imaginary or semi-imaginary characters in a society that has actually existed and that the author is attempting to re-create with some "solidity of specification"[38] from his own experience of observing it or from some close equivalent thereof. One such equivalent would be "the hours of research, the weary 'museum feet'" that Theda Kenyon says "lurk behind" most conventional historical novels.[39] Comparable research may also be necessary to produce John Hersey's "novel of contemporary history."[40] Frye mentions Defoe, Fielding, Austen, and James as central to his tradition of the true novel.

To provide a category for much fiction that preceded the rise of the novel, flourished alongside it in earlier periods, still occasionally competes with it, and has more often mated with it to produce both vigorous and anemic hybrids, Frye proposes to salvage the term "romance" from the littered closet of put-by critical nomenclature, to dust it and demoth it, to sew back some of its lost buttons, and to patch it up thoroughly for long-time use. "It is in the romance," he remarks, "that we find Jung's libido, anima, and shadow reflected in the hero, heroine, and villain respectively." These "psychological archetypes" are nearer the gods of myth than the "real people" of the novel; in their world "the tragic emotions of passion and fury" "can be safely accommodated. . . . So can the supernatural, or the suggestion of it, which is difficult to get into a novel." Emily Brontë and Haw-thorne are foremost among the writers who have impressed Frye as realizing for modern readers the possibilities of the romance. He also includes such an allegory as Bunyan's *The Pilgrim's Progress*, referring to its "revolutionary approach to religious experience."[41]

To meet the difficulty posed by partly fictitious autobiography and partly autobiographical fiction—much of the latter subordi-nating social reality and external nature to the inner life or stream of consciousness of a central character or sequence of characters—Frye proposes a third category: the "confession." It began with St. Augustine, persisted in Browne's *Religio Medici* and Bunyan's *Grace Abounding,* and with Rousseau and Goethe it established itself as one of the main types of modern literature. Although influenced by the true novel's objectivity, the con-fession never deviated far from its author's own intellectual and spiritual growth as explicit, buried, or fragmented subject. Ulti-mately the species evolved toward Joyce's *A Portrait of the Artist as a Young Man* and the considerable number of twen-tieth-century works that bear resemblances to it.

Frye's fourth category is the "anatomy," distinguished by the kind of deliberate oversimplification and distortion that the intel-lect—with its reductive, analytical incisiveness—imposes on exist-ence when the feelings and their tendency to blur clear outlines into a complex wholeness are transcended and held in abeyance. It is interesting that Frye's own theoretical opus—which argues at once persuasively and disconcertingly that literary criticism rather than literature itself is an organized and teachable body of knowl-edge—should be entitled *Anatomy.*

The anatomy as a species of fiction began with Menippean and Varronian satire. Its classical masters were Lucian and Petronius. Its Renaissance masters were Erasmus and Burton and, to a large extent, Rabelais. Its more modern masters have been Swift, Voltaire, the Butler of *Erewhon,* and the Huxley of

Brave New World. Fantasy and moralizing—or "immoralizing"—caricature and erudition, paradox and parody, and what Remy de Gourmont called "the disassociation of ideas" have been its stock in trade. The "anatomist" creates an illusion whose pure form is at the opposite extreme from the verisimilitude of the true novel. He manipulates this illusion to bring ideas to bear on any aspect of life he chooses to simplify and distort.

To these four basic categories—novel, romance, confession, and anatomy—Frye adds others. The most esoteric of his additions may be quickly disposed of. Like everyone else who is honest with himself, Frye doesn't quite know what to do with *Finnegans Wake.* So he takes the unassailable position that into its vast circular abracadabric "riverrun" all four of his basic forms disappear—as into the kind of polar abyss that yawns toward the end of Poe's *Narrative of A. Gordon Pym.* This "fifth and quintessential form," as Frye puts it, "is the one traditionally associated with scriptures and sacred books, and treats life in terms of the fall and awakening of the human soul and the creation and apocalypse of nature." His other examples are the Bible, the Egyptian Book of the Dead, and the Icelandic Prose Edda. He is on somewhat easier ground with *Ulysses,* citing it as the supreme instance of a proper blending—rather than a swallowing up—of novel, romance, confession, and anatomy: "a complete prose epic with all four forms employed in it, all of practically equal importance, and all essential to one another, so that the book is a unity and not an aggregate."[42]

The vast expanse of prose fiction, old and new, that modern critics are just beginning to explore properly, presents—as Frye views it—an embarrassment of riches so far as mixed forms are concerned. Most of these mixtures, however, involve only two or three of his basic forms, rather than all four. Thus there are the romance-novel, as in Conrad's *Lord Jim;* the confession-novel, as in Dorothy Richardson's *Pilgrimage;* the anatomy-novel, as in Huxley's *Point Counter Point;* the romance-confession, as in Borrow's *Lavengro;* the romance-anatomy, as in Melville's *Moby Dick;* and the confession-anatomy, as in Carlyle's *Sartor Resartus.* As for the combinations of three, it is safer to let Frye speak for himself: "we can see strains of novel, romance, and confession in *Pamela,* of novel, romance, and anatomy in *Don Quixote,* of novel, confession, and anatomy in Proust, and of romance, confession, and anatomy in Apuleius."[43]

Finally, Frye has found that each of his basic forms of extended prose fiction has its shorter counterpart—the novel has the more "realistic" short story; the romance, the tale; the confession, the familiar essay; and the anatomy, the dialogue. These also, one presumes, are capable of being mixed, so that one is left wandering through a labyrinthine prose-fiction universe. Its curiously inter-twining stars, planets, moons, comets, asteroids, rings of nebulae, and the pullulating Great White Way itself constitute a mélange that is more than Copernican—it is rather a joint production of Einstein and Disney.

Approached in the light of Frye's categories, Cabell's "Biography" as a whole begins to make aesthetic sense—a sense that has never penetrated the literal-mindedness of some of his critics. Only in his fictions dealing with relatively modern times has Cabell approached the novel or the realistic short story, and even these are more accurately described as romance-novels and semi-tales, with some elements of the confession and the familiar essay. Most of the "Biography" avoids the novel and its shorter equivalent. All the major fictions dealing with the past represent the threefold synthesis that Frye finds best exemplified in Apuleius' *The Golden Ass*. In other words, they are blendings of romance, confession, and anatomy. They make extensive use of myths, legends, and folk tales drawn from standard dictionaries and encyclopedias of such material and from such retellings for popular consumption as S. Baring-Gould's *Curious Myths of the Middle Ages* and *Legends of the Patriarchs and Prophets* and W. R. S. Ralston's *Russian Folk Tales*.[44] In this respect the world they unfold has many points of resemblance to the world of Lord Dunsany's fictions.

As for the prologue and epilogue—*Beyond Life* and *Straws and Prayer-Books*—these are confession-anatomies, compounded of familiar essays and dialogues. Such items as the running commentary of the prefaces, the extended introduction to the genealogy in *The Lineage of Lichfield*, and some of the appendices, are familiar essays, with *Taboo* functioning as a straight Swiftian anatomy. The poems of *From the Hidden Way* and the play *The Jewel Merchants* are thrown in for good measure. Thus considered, the "Biography" becomes one of the most elaborate experiments with Frye's forms of fiction in all twentieth-century literature.

Cabell always insisted that he should never be read or judged

primarily as a novelist. This is the point of the elaborate derogation of all forms of so-called "realistic" fiction in *Beyond Life*,
reaching its climax in the ingenious demonstration that Flaubert
in *Madame Bovary*—precisely because of his inhuman clinical
objectivity—"is refining phrases about a collocation outside of
human experience."[45] The arguments against the novel in *Beyond Life* lean heavily on Stevenson's many excursions into
criticism, such as "A Note on Realism," "A Gossip on Romance,"
and "A Humble Remonstrance"; on Oscar Wilde's "The Decay
of Lying" in *Intentions;* and on Arthur Machen's *Hieroglyphics*.[46]

To look beyond the "Biography" proper for a moment, one
of Cabell's most revealing discussions of romance is in the essay
on Elinor Wylie entitled "Sanctuary in Porcelain" in *Some of
Us*. In this essay he distinguishes between two kinds—"that major
romance which gilds actuality with the gold of a highly superior
sun, as opposed to that minor romance over which one is tempted
to say the moon presides. . . ." Although both are preferable
to the novel, he has a liking for the minor kind which "embellishes life because the writer has found life to be unendurably
ugly." "Its goals are not of this world. It does not hunt the
improbable: it evokes in desperation that which it over well
knows to be impossible."[47]

This desperate romance is the last resort of the imagination
in an age of science and journalism. In "The Nightmare Has
Triplets," the forest of Branlon symbolizes the place of last
resort for "each minor poet."[48] When Smire confronts "the public
at large," he insists that "romance" and "novel" be sharply
separated:

> So does this widespread confusion of two different forms of art
> force me to suggest that all fiction should be divided, rigorously,
> into two classes: the fiction of the novelist, who, almost always
> in prose, reproduces human life as it is, or as it has been, lived
> in some actual era; and the fiction of the romancer, who, whether
> it be in prose or in verse, reproduces human life in a cosmos
> invented—or, to speak more strictly, "compiled," or it may be
> merely "rearranged"—by the author of this fiction.[49]

When he returns from Branlon—walking jauntily along the
gray beaches of Acheron, from which one ferries to the world
of science and journalism—Smire encounters nine derisive spectres "masquerading, in long gowns made out of provincial news-

papers, as the Nine Muses." They cry out that Branlon is " 'de-cadent nostalgia,' " " 'pastiche,' " and " 'old hat.' " They point out that in Branlon " 'there is no class struggle,' " " 'one does not face the realities of life,' " and " 'there is no grave consideration of such modern problems as most deeply intrigue the intelligent-sia during this week-end.' " Hence Branlon is " 'sophomoric,' " " 'does not reflect the American scene fearlessly,' " and is " 'pseudo this, and pseudo that, but above all . . . pseudo the other.' " When Smire attempts to cow them with an animal parable and some of Stevenson's phrases, they do not subside sheepishly but try to hog the argument by derogatory, dissenting grunts. Then, breaking out in "thin laughter," they screech in unison: " 'Now, but this absurd out-of-date creature is telling us, yet again, that the dream is better than the reality!' " Whereupon Smire-Cabell replies to his critics: " 'To the contrary, I am telling you that for humankind the dream is the one true reality.' "[50]

Cabell best sums up his animus against the novel in two defi-nitions. One occurs in *Beyond Life:* " 'Realism' is the art of being superficial seriously."[51] The other is in *Smirt,* where liter-ary naturalism is referred to by one of its youthful exponents as "a very lusty bastard begotten upon realism with the phallus of agony."[52] Despite this animus, however, Cabell prefers sincere novelists of the "realistic" or "naturalistic" schools to the ven-dors of the sort of formulae romance in novel form that panders to the public at large. Perhaps Charteris devotes an excessive amount of space to such vendor-panders in *Beyond Life,* spend-ing some of his best wit to bestow an invidious distinction on names now as forgotten as those of Harold Bell Wright and Syd-nor Harrison. Also, in major fictions of the "Biography"—as will be indicated in more detail later—Cabell the anatomist relies on the reader's familiarity with and acceptance of the novel to have fun with some of the most cherished conventions of Cabell the romancer.

In the "Biography" viewed as a whole, however, the greatest literary fun arises from the pervasive flouting of the novel in its most naturalistic form. The saga of the life of Manuel, indeed, may be regarded as an extended parody of the Rougon-Macquart series of Émile Zola.[53] In twenty documentary novels Zola traces hereditary "lesions" of the nervous system through several gen-erations of "low mimetic"[54] characters under the pretext of being thoroughly scientific. In romance-confession-anatomies that exploit Erich Fromm's "forgotten language" of ancient fantasies rather than "facts," and that add up also "to a neat twenty,"[55] Cabell shows the transmission of his chivalrous, gallant, and poetic attitudes through many more generations of "high mimetic"[56] characters. No one can say that he has neglected the proletariat and the bourgeoisie, however, since Manuel was once a swineherd, his Niafer served as a kitchen wench, and Jurgen came to be a pawnbroker. Although the premises of science about human life—or inferences drawn from these premises—intrude often into the thoughts and speeches of the characters, the illusion is that of a nonsense world of pre-scientific irreality, while the schema and style of the whole derive primarily from poetry and the fine arts.

VI *The Axis of the Arts*

Approached from this last point of view, the "Biography"—despite its flouting of the novel—has an interesting nexus with one of the main directions that the novel-form has taken in the modern world. Shortly after the turn of the century, the novelist was confronted with three possibilities. Zola, who had sought to relate the form to science, enjoined his disciples to adopt from specific sciences their methods of gathering factual data and likewise their developing codifications of "truths," of emergent inferences and verified hypotheses. His reliance on effects borrowed from impressionist painting was a saving grace, which twentieth-century criticism has discovered.[57] H. G. Wells, with a humility as impudently flaunted as Zola's arrogance, guided the novel in the direction of journalism. He conceived the form as a forum for the agitation of issues that the march of events had infused with urgency. Averse to either of these vulgarizations, Henry James strove in both his theory and practice to keep the novel—already endowed with an ethos and a cultural instrumentality by the great Victorians, the French, and the Russians—within the vivid and beautiful axis of the arts, moving it simultaneously toward picture and toward drama.

James's fusion of drama with picture led to the stream-of-consciousness novel, which added the emphases of lyrical poetry and music. These emphases lent unusual distinction to the work of James Joyce, Dorothy Richardson, Marcel Proust, Virginia Woolf, and Elizabeth Bowen. A novelist like E. M. Forster, who did not share James's preoccupation with the technical problem of "point of view,"[58] nevertheless experimented with musical devices to implement his theory of "rhythm." The so-called "impressionism" of Ford Madox Ford and Joseph Conrad—representing another solution to the problem of "point of view" than that exhibited in stream-of-consciousness fiction—was "painterly" with a vengeance, as Marlow and Dowell did their brush strokes. Novelists of ideas like André Gide and Aldous Huxley sought to achieve "the musicalization of fiction" in the fugue-structures of *The Counterfeiters* and *Point Counter Point,* and Huxley in *Antic Hay* borrowed from the dance. Romain Rolland's *Jean-Christophe* imitated symphonic form; Franz Werfel's *Verdi,* operatic form. D. H. Lawrence's psychological and cultural primitivism found expression in prose as hectic as the rhythms of tribal fornication rituals and as vivid as a canvas by Gauguin. Graham Greene turned to cinema, producing effects that make his serious novels more exciting than his "entertainments." Expressionist drama had its impact on Franz Kafka and Alfred Döblin, as it had on Joyce. The superimposition of the art of the cartoon upon the art of the stained-glass window individualized the fiction of Ronald Firbank. The powerful visual imaginations of Ernest Hemingway and William Faulkner—disciplined by the "objective correlatives," imagery, and unorthodox tersenesses and turgidities of modern metaphysical poetry—created, respectively, new models of classical and baroque prose in the novel.

Much of this experimentation left Cabell cold. Of some of it, too, he remained unaware, for *avant-garde* literature often bored him intolerably. The stream-of-consciousness novel in the Joyce and Proust traditions was one of his aversions. Abundance of concrete visual detail he apparently associated with the scientific documentation of the naturalistic novel. He could imitate the usual stream-of-consciousness tricks as well as the naturalistic gambit of cataloguing particulars, when, as in "The Nightmare Has Triplets," his chief purpose was parody. But in the characteristic narrative of the "Biography" he shuns both. When he does experiment there with the recording of a character's inner life over a considerable period of time—as in the treatment of Coth of the Rocks in *The Silver Stallion*—he prefers an odd use of the second-person along with the third-person, balancing empathy and detachment.

The relation of his more ornate impressionistic writing or

"purple patches," however, to aureate illustration is apparent—as, for example, in the remarkable chapter entitled "Confusions of the Golden Travel" in *Something About Eve.* This and comparable passages are exercises in cadenced contrapuntal prose.[59] They employ brocaded diction, alliteration, assonance, repetition or refrain, in striking ways. They are a kind of plated rhetorical poetry that is the diametrical opposite of the conversational idiom that the modern ear usually prefers in both poetry and prose.[60] Frequently these exercises are the monologues of characters in moments of either reverie or action. Sometimes they are the omniscient author's intrusive embellishments. Also, there are hidden indulgences in more metrical verse-making—particularly hexameters—and even buried parodies of poets.[61]

By far, however, the most impressive relation of the "Biography" as a whole to the axis of the arts is in its total schema. Cabell treats his three attitudes as musical themes or motifs, introducing one after the other, blending and contrasting and expanding and developing them in always-flowing time, and at last recapitulating the triad with new variations and a coda of return to the point of outset. The analogy is with symphony[62]— on a vaster scale than Romain Rolland achieved in the form of the symbolic-realistic novel, and daedalianly complicated by the commingling elaboration of the comedic and the fluvial metaphors. Above the dark river's endless ocean-hungry gurgle, beyond the constant dance of bright evanescent ripples, hovers jauntily a jester's cap and bells—forever jingling in the wind.

CHAPTER 3

The Way of Chivalry

I *Figures of Earth*

IN A MINOR EPISODE about halfway through *Figures of Earth*, first major romance of the "Biography," the protagonist Dom Manuel—now a count whose fief is still in a usurper's hands —is leaving one of his momentary loves, Queen Freydis, to bring back from the dead the kitchen-wench Niafer, with whom he had fallen truly in love on his first adventure as a swineherd turned knight-errant. At the outskirts of the forest in which he is to attempt this resurrection, he encounters a knight whose armor is vermilion and who wears a woman's sleeve in his helmet. This exponent of the chivalrous code of woman-worship wishes to know the name of Manuel's ladylove. When Manuel replies that he has none living except the woman he has just unceremoniously deserted, the vermilion fanatic tells him his conduct is an ill-seeming violation of chivalry's way. Manuel replies: " 'Very probably you are right, but I am not chivalrous. I am Manuel. I follow after my own thinking. . . .' "[1] After further verbal exchanges—in the course of which Manuel reveals too much about himself—he has to slay the knight who is in reality a black sandman with a red mouse for a soul.

This episode makes very clear that Manuel, although he is to be the founder of Poictesme's great chivalric Fellowship of the Silver Stallion—an order comparable to the Arthurian Round Table or Charlemagne's inner circle—is not, midway in his career, fully conscious of the code he is to serve but is basically a stubborn egoist who is hell-bent on accomplishing certain objectives that he believes are peculiarly his in this life. He may thus be described not as a conventionally chivalrous hero at all but as the kind of simple-minded idealist out of whose obstinacies and blunderings and unscrupulosities a sort of earthly success ensues, a chivalrous myth is made, and even a religion is born or bolstered or broadcast.

The mock-medieval world that is the setting of his experiences is composed of so many esoteric places and is so abundant in supernatural and preternatural creatures and their goings-on that to try to describe it as if it constituted an order or cosmos would be vain and misleading. But certain facts and personages of this world do emerge as more immediately important for Manuel than are others.

The basic fact is a mysterious law of recurrence that is neither Plato's nor Nietzsche's but vaguely suggests both. The means by which Cabell conveys this principle is to have the ending of Manuel's adventures suddenly become their re-beginning and to imply that even their beginning was close on the ending of those of a still older Manuel. In the last chapter the aged Manuel is gazing into the river of Lethe. Images of his whole life appear, swept away "like bright broken wreckage."[2] Grandfather Death, who has accompanied him to this last place, untethers the vicious swine of Eubouleus. Forthwith the scene blurs. The river of Lethe changes to the first chapter's pool of Haranton, wherein strange dreams engender, and beside which are the miller's harmless pigs and the figure of a man that young Manuel has shaped from clay. Speaking is Miramon Lluagor, "lord of the nine kinds of sleep and prince of the seven madnesses,"[3] Grandfather Death's half-brother, who has come in disguise to awaken Manuel to his first quest. Manuel replies thus to the speaker's remarks about the water. " '. . . there, where it should reflect the remnants of the old fellow that is I, it shows, instead, the face of a young boy who is used to following after his own thinking and his own desires.' " Miramon then observes, as he did in Chapter I: " 'Certainly it is queer you should be saying that; for that, as everybody knows, was the favorite byword of your namesake the famous Count Manuel who is so newly dead in Poictesme yonder. . . .' "[4]

Although Miramon later serves in the Fellowship of the Silver Stallion, he is more an arbiter than a subordinate of Manuel's world. Not only is he responsible for Manuel's start in knight-errantry, but he also engineers his conquest of Poictesme. Above Miramon, however, are his half-brother Death and their reputedly insane coadjutor, Horvendile. For these two force the young

Manuel to choose between his own life and that of his beloved Niafer; then they materially assist Miramon in helping Manuel to supreme power, and finally manage Manuel's disillusioned passing. Still another arbiter is the trunkless head known variously as Béda, Krushina, Mimir, or Misery, whom Manuel must serve for a month of years in order to bring Niafer back from her pagan paradise, and who is one agent of Manuel's ultimate disillusionment with his existence. A world in which Death, Sleep, Madness, and Misery preside, and conspire together to control and shroud in mystery the approaches to deeper truth and reality, is anything but a consoling one.

This generally ghoulish masculine quartet of arbiters is counterpointed by a more pleasant quartet of women who represent the ideals that enter into Manuel's experience. The first of these is the mysterious Suskind, who is not a figure of earth and with whom Manuel trysts at twilight in the wood before Miramon seeks him out to send him on his first ambiguous quest. In the end Manuel is compelled to murder her lest she bewitch and destroy the normality of his eldest and best-loved daughter. Suskind is the divine discontent, the memory of the lost innocence of another world, that he who seeks to make a figure in this world—and to preserve the symbols of this world's success —must ruthlessly put behind him to his ultimate regret.

The second woman is the kitchen-wench Niafer, who in the guise of a boy accompanies young Manuel as an apparent rival on his first quest and astonishes him by the cleverness that is not really hers. When the quest's outcome leaves him ridiculous, he turns to Niafer as something real and dear to offset fraud and scorn. When he is faced with his own death unless he gives her up, self-preservation prevails. But she so haunts him even in the company of other, more beautiful, more accomplished women that he is finally willing to suffer grievously to have her back and keep her always, though she returns—in consequence of his impaired memory—as a lame parody of her former self. She is the ideal of connubial and domestic contentment, to whom he who seeks to make a figure in the world reverts inevitably with a sentiment that conquers rationality.

The third woman is the Princess Alianora; in the disguise of a swan-maiden, she visits Manuel at the pool of Haranton when he returns there after the fraud of his first quest and the cruel loss of Niafer. The magic feather that Alianora manages to lose to him as a passport and a lure—even though it is destroyed—serves its purpose. It inspires him—along with the memory of Niafer's coached cleverness—to play the mountebank successfully and to win finally the wealth and title that permit him to enjoy Alianora's passion on a more equal social basis. Because she desires him physically, she prevents his deceptions from being discovered. Considerably, then, to her collusion and lust he owes his ultimate success. She marries the King of England for political reasons, but Manuel returns to her, even when he is past his prime, for one last adulterous indulgence of his youthful ardor. She is the ideal of sexual excitement that the strong man cannot renounce and for which on occasion he will even betray his marriage vows. But in preferring Niafer to Alianora and in letting Alianora go so that he can seek out Queen Freydis, Manuel tests the way of gallantry and finds it lacking—for him at least—in abiding significance and appeal.

The last woman, Queen Freydis, is—like Suskind—not of this earth. Hearing that Freydis can impart life to images, Manuel by using magic coaxes her to pass through the fire barrier between her realm of Audela and the realm of ordinary living. She loses her wholly supernal status, yields to Manuel's human love, and animates his inadequate clay sculpture. She represents the ideal of creative inspiration that leaders of men require as well as poets. But Manuel prefers having the lost, real Niafer as flesh and blood again with all her tender bossiness rather than seeing any more of his artifices quickened into morbid, amoral life. When Freydis tells him that he can perform this miracle only by paying a price to Misery, he leaves her for Misery's service.

Even when he has Niafer back and is reasonably content with her, however, he must still rely on Freydis. He brings Niafer to Freydis so that the latter can help them have children after the stork fashion approved in Philistia, from whose Queen Stultitia Manuel has been hoping to secure military assistance. Freydis meanwhile has been aiding as well as harrying other image-makers and has taken as consort Manuel's first created godling, Sesphra—or Phrases—who winds up as one of a trinity worshiped in Philistia; the others are Vel-Tyno, or Novelty, and Ageus, or Usage. This trinity of the Philistines—the equivalent of America's faddism, conformism, and sloganeering, or, in more recent terminology, its waste-making, status-seeking, and hidden persuasions—is antithetical to what Freydis really stands for. But the decadent Sesphra fascinates Manuel and nearly persuades him to murder Niafer and her first child. Freydis intervenes, though not for strictly moral reasons. She and Manuel then part forever, for Manuel has gained as much from her creativity as he now feels he needs. His relationship with Freydis has emphasized the conflict in his nature between the poetic attitude and the imperatives of the man of action.

Figures of Earth—as has been indicated earlier—is subtitled *A Comedy of Appearances,* and this subtitle is undoubtedly the clue to its main theme. Stressed in Manuel's initiation quest and in his recovery from its results are not only the discrepancies between appearance and reality but also the dominance and triumph of appearance. The world deceives, but it also wishes to be deceived.

The stranger who brings Manuel the magic sword, and inspires him to use it to rescue the princess supposedly carried off by the cruel wizard, is the wizard himself. The princess is in reality the wizard's too high-spirited wife, who bores him and of whom he cannot be rid unless some champion takes her away according to the conventions of romance. The sword is of no use against the monsters who guard the mountain approaches to the wizard's palace, since Manuel's rival easily disposes of them by his clever trickery. The rival turns out to be the servant girl sent for by the wizard's wife, and even the servant girl's cleverness is a cheat. The wizard is not too much concerned about being slain, since he is a semi-immortal. The wizard's wife, instead of wanting to be rescued from her husband or having any interest in her champion, angrily demands the magic sword from Manuel and ridicules his swineherd's rags.

Those monsters desisted from attacking Manuel and Niafer because each believed an ordinary object to be a magic one. Hence a feather from an ordinary goose is just as effective in leading Manuel to Alianora as the destroyed magic swan feather. The foolish Helmas accepts one goose feather as an omen of wisdom, the evil Ferdinand another goose feather as an omen of holiness; and by playing up to the qualities that thus come to be expected of them—by what appears to be the true fulfillment of a prophecy—they actually acquire some measure of these qualities. The coming of Manuel with his third goose feather enables Alianora to enjoy her lust for him under the

appearance of predestined love. The accidents and blunders of
Manuel's past fall into a pattern that permits him to appear
to others and to believe himself that he is the redeemer of
Poictesme—one comparable to Mithras, Huitzilopochtli, Tam-
mouz, Heracles, Gautama, Dionysos, and Krishna—and the force
of these combined illusions helps catapult him to such eminence.
Just as Miramon Lluagor, the lord of illusion, dwells at the sum-
mit of Vraidex, the mountain of truth, so is all experience a
tissue of ambiguous dualisms—of folly masquerading as wisdom,
evil as holiness, lust as love, failure as success.

The full meaning of this latter dualism does not come home to
Manuel until near the end of his career. Then, in the study of his
palace at Storisende, he grasps the same truth about appearances that came to the prisoner in Plato's cave who, becoming
unchained, discovered the real status of the shadows on the
wall. The solid world of sense itself is revealed as mere appearance—images in a window of Ageus, or usage or customary
human assent. Beyond that window is another reality entirely—
a noumenal chaos and old night inhabited by creatures and
images of pre-existence. Manuel's whole career, his good and evil
deeds, his triumphs and defeats, his ecstasies and miseries—these
have all been for nonexistents in a phenomenal nothingness that,
even as appearance, must soon pass away. The same profoundly
disturbing awareness—so the preface tells us—came to Cabell
himself one fine afternoon in 1919 at the window of his study
at Dumbarton Grange, and out of this moment of either mysticism
or indigestion grew "the 80,000 words or so" of *Figures of Earth*.[5]

But another subtitle than *Comedy of Appearances* might have
been used, with equal and perhaps truer relevance to the book's
final meaning. *Figures of Earth* is also a comedy of obligations,
which are among its appearances—and its realities! Manuel may
think he is following his own thinking and desires, but actually
he spends most of his time trying to live up to one or another
obligation that somebody else has put upon him. He has an
obligation to his mother to make a figure in the world and to
give it life. He has an obligation to Niafer to make amends for
letting Grandfather Death take her in his stead—to bring her
back into warm flesh, to provide her with children, a pedigree,
a position, and a home. He has obligations to his allies and fol-
lowers to live up to the messianic destiny Miramon has discovered in his past, and to Alianora to come to her arms when

she sends her talisman, and to his daughter Melicent to save her from the spell of Suskind. When Grandfather Death comes for him—confronting him with the final undeniable evidence of his failure and his unimportance—he has an obligation to the figure he has made in the world to defend his success and, even when he chooses to accompany Death, to remind him that "'in Poictesme the Count of Poictesme goes first in any company.'"[6] For him to be keeping up appearances at such a moment has its comic but also its sublime side. In short, he goes to the river of Lethe and the swine of Eubouleus with a final dignity that is not mere appearance.

One of the defects of *Figures of Earth* is an episodic action that makes for a loose rather than a firm structure. Cabell seeks to impose an appearance of firmness on this recalcitrant structure by a controlling metaphor of accounting that is appropriate to a romance of success. Thus the episodes unfold in five books entitled "Credit," "Spending," "Cast Accounts," "Surcharge," and "Settlement." When the settlement is reached, there may be material but not spiritual bankruptcy. Manuel, by living up to virtually all his obligations, has proved himself admirable and hence chivalrous in a deeper sense than he himself ever realized or than had ever entered into the code thinking of the spruce vermilion knight.

II *The Silver Stallion*

The Silver Stallion, the second major romance of the "Biography," throws further revealing—and, in large measure, iconoclastic—light on the genesis of the way of chivalry as a heritage from feudal times. *The Silver Stallion*, which has even less unity of action than *Figures of Earth* and lacks the integrative principle of a central character, is, indeed, a framework assortment of tales held together thematically—as is Sherwood Anderson's *Winesburg, Ohio*, Thornton Wilder's *The Bridge of San Luis Rey*, or William Faulkner's *The Unvanquished*.

The iconoclasm is pervasive and occurs on several levels. The first level concerns the Fellowship of the Silver Stallion before it was disbanded. In *Figures of Earth* the Fellowship, for the most part in the background, was referred to as one of the factors in Manuel's achievement of the physical redemption of Poictesme. *The Silver Stallion* begins with the disbanding of this

Fellowship after Manuel's passing and follows in detail the destinies of seven of its nine members. As the reader delves into these seven champions' destinies, he learns a good deal about the past of each. A composite picture of the Fellowship in its prime emerges, and this portrayal is not a pretty one. It was a gang of hellions who, under the pretexts of patriotism, justice, and robust recreation, perpetrated tyranny, murder, pillage, fornication, drunkenness, and other outrages.

The second level of iconoclasm concerns the image of Manuel which the huge statue surmounting his empty tomb symbolizes and the piety and poetry of the realm conspire to promulgate. The image is that of a Christian warrior and a paragon of all the noble virtues who was always profound in intelligence and vision and always clear and firm in purpose. The great purpose now attributed to him is eventual return as a messiah to accomplish the spiritual redemption of the Poictesme that he and his Fellowship redeemed physically. The basis for believing that he intends to return is a story told by the boy Jurgen, son of the most stubborn ruffian among all the champions—Coth of the Rocks. Jurgen made up the story to save himself from another of Coth's spankings, the last of which inspired him to run away from home and stay out all the night when Manuel—as his daughter Melicent reported—rode westward with Grandfather Death.

Here, in other words, is a religious myth glorifying Manuel as the very kind of chivalrous hero he fell far short of being. If his widow Niafer had not fallen under the influence of Holy Holmendis—a saint from Philistia—this myth would not perhaps have grown so quickly. But with Holmendis' zeal to spread it for his own interests—and with the aid of the universal human tendency to wish to be deceived by appearances and to believe because it is absurd—the myth acquires a potency that is soon reshaping the mores of Poictesme beyond recognition.

The importance of the subtitle—*A Comedy of Redemption*—should thus be clear. It becomes clearer as one moves to the third level of iconoclasm, which concerns the destinies of seven of the nine champions after the disbanding of the Fellowship. These seven and Manuel's image are the protagonists of *The Silver Stallion*. So far as the seven are concerned, the book might have been subtitled—almost as appropriately—"A Comedy of Nemesis." The disbanding itself means that the hellions are to tame down considerably and that some are to suffer dooms peculiarly appropriate to the lives they have led. The myth affects them in various and ironical ways: only one sincerely believes it; the others divide equally into disbelievers and false believers. Although all seven pursue their dooms without real amendment of their former selves, the myth with its chivalrous virtues draws them, willy-nilly, into the glorious web-work of its rank imposture; transfigured, they pass with Manuel into the selective memory of posterity.

But though nemesis, as embodied in the prescient and pitiless intrusions of Horvendile, and iconoclasm, as stressed at the end by Niafer's shaken faith and by the middle-aged Jurgen's cynical pragmatism, appear to dominate this comedy, another emphasis keeps intruding: a muted, intermittent, and yet unmistakable counterpoint. When Coth at long last gains audience with Manuel in the heathen land of the dead and implores him to return to Poictesme for the purpose of destroying his false image and denying his messianic role, Manuel reproves the old realist for his stubborn stupidity and tells him that the myth is better. Even though Holmendis' and Dame Niafer's zeal leads them into excesses of reform, the younger generation—as a result of the myth—begins to show traits that have hitherto been rare or nonexistent in either the young or the adult: civility, forgiveness, respect for others' property, even some measure of sobriety and chastity. The result is an undeniable increase in social tranquility and personal happiness.

Despite the fact that none of the seven champions is ever regenerated, each elicits from the reader a modicum of sympathy—even, perhaps, a touch of admiration. Gonfal might have wed Queen Morvyth, whom he had won through chicanery and other means from all her suitors; but he declines to temporize with the integrity and consistency of his skeptical philosophy, although not to do so means his beheading. Miramon might have changed the status quo of his entire destiny, but he prefers to retain it because he cannot do without either his art for art's sake or his wife. Coth has such an affection for the vices of the Manuel he remembers that he is willing to go to the ends of the earth to make this personal image prevail over the public one that has been falsified and defiled by virtues. Guivic, finding himself dispossessed of his body by the salvation-hungry Sylvan, uses the incubus status to which he is relegated through their trade, as an instrument for increasing the sum of women's pleasure.

Kerin, after finding through long study underground the same disillusioning truth that his wife has arrived at by another kind of application, prefers to flout his conclusions with the faith that sustains. Ninzian is sincere in his remorse for having been delinquent in his duties to Lucifer, does not lose confidence in the confessional discretion of his wife, is happy with Lucifer to discover that God is being a good sportsman in respecting the rules of the game they are playing for human souls, but is slightly shocked that his master Lucifer should refer to him as a hypocrite rather than as a leader of reform. Finally, when Donander—through an error in supernatural efficiency and by virtue of his superlative physical attractiveness—rises above Paradise to become the last practicing God in a universe rid of humanity, the human heart at least survives in his continued faith in the Manuelian myth of Christian chivalry. Each in his way is an idealist with a core of dignity.

In *Figures of Earth* the anatomist in Cabell led him to launch satire from Poictesme at the gods of twentieth-century America, and also at American optimism concerning World War I, in his treatment of Manuel's campaign against the Northmen as "a war to end war forever."[7] This kind of anatomizing is even more frequent in *The Silver Stallion,* where there are slightly concealed quips at such *bêtes noires* of Menckenian iconoclasm as southern fundamentalism, Calvin Coolidge,[8] Prohibition, Puritanism, Philistinism, and reform. The presence of so much topical innuendo—along with bawdry similarly managed—adds to the variety but perhaps not to the aesthetic coherence of an already sufficiently complex comedy.

III *Domnei and The Way of Ecben*

The chivalrous attitude achieves its complete and, on the whole, victorious expression in two shorter romances: the first, *Domnei,* subtitled *A Comedy of Woman-Worship;* the second, *The Way of Ecben,* subtitled *A Comedietta Involving a Gentleman.* Structurally, *Domnei* is considerably less episodic than either *Figures of Earth* or *The Silver Stallion;* indeed, it comes close to having the organic action of a well-made melodrama. Action, however, is subordinated in *Domnei* to the characters who, in turn, precipitate and to some extent control it as it moves forward: hence the titles of each of the four parts—"Perion," "Melicent," "Demetrios," and "Ahasuerus." In *The Way of Ecben* the gentleman, King Alfgar, makes a renunciation, survives a strenuous journey to the goal he has set himself, and has his supreme moment of triumph before being suddenly destroyed. The action proceeds straightforwardly in four uncomplicated linear movements, with an epilogue.

In *Domnei*, Perion, the young virtuous outlaw, and Melicent, the beautiful eldest daughter of Dom Manuel and Niafer, fall ideally in love at first sight, after the approved fashion of romantic lovers. In the way of their love, circumstance opposes a series of obstacles—some conventional, others bizarrely Cabellian—which they seek to overcome with the sort of superhuman effort and undeviating faith that no artistry can make very convincing. The reader, in other words, has to surrender to the mood of one who believes in a creed because it is absurd. Only then can he willingly suspend his disbelief in the fictive world of *Domnei*.

Physical passion and the mere bodily chastity that is so highly esteemed by men under the double standard of morality recede in importance before spiritual love and fidelity. The woman will endure any kind of degradation and submit to death itself for the welfare of her knight, for she trusts Christian Providence to provide compensation for her ordeals and sacrifices. Her faith to her pledged word is obsessional to the point of fantastically ironical folly. To win possession of her against all obstacles is the penultimate step toward that union with the divine sought by the mystic in his life's pilgrimage. The knight, of course, relies on feats of arms and the strength to withstand all manner of external perils rather than on the persistent soul-searching of the mystic. At the last, however, it is an inward miracle that must bolster him against disillusionment—Time's secret weapon.

The main foe of Perion and Melicent for most of the action is Demetrios of Anatolia, son of Miramon Lluagor—the wizard who played so important a role in both *Figures of Earth* and *The Silver Stallion*. By the decree of the Norns or Fates, which Miramon chose not to set aside when he had the power, Demetrios slew his father, kept his magic sword Flamberge, and became a bulwark of paganism. He makes Perion his captive and slave. To ransom Perion, Melicent must enter Demetrios' harem.

Even though the beastly pagan takes her virginity, he cannot touch her soul. This defeat irks his inordinate pride, and this irked pride causes him to behave most inconsistently and ironically. Perion wounds him mortally in combat, and Demetrios' own son Oedipus speeds his demise.

Demetrios is more than a beastly villain providing a melodramatic obstacle to the course of true love. Cabell intellectualizes him into a complex, extreme exponent of the way of gallantry. His inability to comprehend the criteria that determine the conduct of Melicent and Perion toward him and toward each other over long years is an amusing commentary on the inadequacies of his own code and credo. As he goes baffled to his death, he is the comic butt of chivalry's Platonic-Christian geste.

Lurking in the background is the treacherous Jew, Ahasuerus, who at first served Perion, later serves Demetrios, and then Oedipus; he is revealed as a betrayer of all his masters in order to have Melicent for himself. When he has her in his power and she is willing to yield her body to him to keep the bargain she has made to save Perion, Ahasuerus surprises the reader by displaying a pride greater even than that of Demetrios. All along the Jew has played the pimp, the voyeur, and the intriguer because he is enamored—not of her body—but of her soul. Foiled by her integrity, he consoles himself by arranging for Perion to win her back. Thus the Jew thinks that he has won by usurping the role of Providence.

Again, Cabell has transformed a melodramatic villain by the superimposition of allegory. Ahasuerus is the incarnation of the diabolism that haunted Cabell himself. In a way that gallantry cannot, this diabolism comprehends the inner force of Christian spirituality and idealism; but it tries to pervert this force because of the envy engendered by fallen angelhood or discipleship. In such a futile endeavor, diabolism also becomes a comic butt of the Platonic-Christian geste.

If Demetrios can be said to illustrate Cabell's use of the myth of the anti-Christ, Ahasuerus represents his use of the myth of the Wandering Jew. Through Cabell's ironic treatment of Ahasuerus and Demetrios, both myths contribute to a laughter of gayety as Perion—at first disappointed to find that the Melicent he has won at long last is not the Melicent of his first devotion—

feels the upthrust of a wholly new devotion, a maturer and sublimer passion.

Rather than gayety, a high sobriety pervades *The Way of Ecben*. The renunciation made by King Alfgar of Ecben, the protagonist of this romance, is drastic in its idealism. A mature rather than a youthful exponent of chivalry, he gives his crown and Ettaine, his queen-to-be, to King Ulf of Rorn, his conquered enemy, and then sets out to find the Garden between Dawn and Sunrise. His motivation is a vision of Ettarre, Dom Manuel's youngest daughter, whom the poet Madoc brought back from the wasteland behind the moon and to whose never-dying beauty Horvendile is dedicated, although he can never possess her. As Alfgar journeys toward the garden to win Ettarre, he must undergo trials devised by Time's leper avatars to test his allegiance to his king, his god, and his lady in fealty or—as Cabell prefers to express it—"in domnei." He survives each trial but with physical losses, so that he at last approaches the garden with all the impairments of age—shrivelled hands, deafness, and blindness.

Attendant upon Ettarre is Horvendile, representing diabolism in conjunction with the poetic attitude and the ideal beauty that inspires it; and these two epitomize the Cabellian aesthetic. Neither can at first comprehend the nature and the criteria of this madman Alfgar. With eloquent dialectic they seek to make him aware of his folly and futility. But the faith of Alfgar is indissuadable. So Divine Providence and Grace—or, it may be, the Norns, since there is no use trying to figure out the ultimate mystery of Cabell's cosmos—reward him by restoring him to his youth and by preparing for his nuptials with the lady of his vision. Horvendile joins the other celebrating poets in the garden and comes forth to be best man, although he smacks unmistakably of Ahasuerus, as well as Madoc. Then, having granted Alfgar his supreme moment, Providence—or the Norn trio—snatches him away to salvation or oblivion through the agency of the revengeful gods of Rorn. He had angered them by his long opposition and his obstinate profession of belief in his own god of Ecben, even though he knew that his god had been superseded.

King Alfgar achieves the full chivalrous dignity that shone only partially through Manuel's last disillusionment and through the final choices and gestures of the seven champions of *The Silver Stallion*.

IV *Chivalry and The Line of Love*

The ten tales gathered into *Chivalry* and three of the nine
tales that constitute *The Line of Love* trace manifestations of
the way of chivalry from the thirteenth to the sixteenth centuries. The entire group cannot be said to add a great deal to the
understanding of chivalry's tenets afforded by *Domnei* and *The
Way of Ecben*. Nor is much originality or variety in the handling
of the shorter form of the tale apparent. Aureate description,
dialogue more artificial than Cabell usually writes, and songs
sung by characters at appropriate moments are some of the
recurrent technical features. Eleven of the tales are attributed to
the imaginary fifteenth-century chronicler Nicolas de Caen. The
narrative perspective of twelve of them is the chronicler's omniscient third person. Only one—supposed to be an autobiographical
fragment left by the chief character—is in first-person narrative.
Melodrama of a somewhat conventional, seldom resourceful type
—using disguise, flight and pursuit, combat, and a suitable frequency of corpses—abounds, but the cadenced prose keeps the
pace from ever becoming really brisk, and the suspense is generally slight and sometimes nonexistent. Although the borrowing
from actual history is more pronounced than in the major comedies or romances so far considered, the treatment of such
material is deliberately cavalier so as to produce the effect of
legend touched by the marvelous. Yet the least of these tales has
minor nuances of theme and style that are of some interest to
the student of Cabell's more mature work.

One function of *Chivalry* is to support the view of Manuel's
return expressed by Freydis and concurred in by Alianora when
they appear in Niafer's dream toward the close of *The Silver
Stallion*. This view rejects messianic supernaturalism and holds
that Manuel will come back, almost to the life, in certain of
his descendants. "The Story of the Tenson" and "The Story of
the Rat-Trap" portray Alianora's son, Edward I of England, as
another Manuel in his physique, his spirit of adventure, his sense
of responsibility to a divine thrusting on, his appeal for women
with a comparable appreciation of their destiny—such as his two
queens, Ellinor and Meregrett—and his cunning in dealing with
political adversaries. "The Story of the Housewife" shows that

Edward III inherits not only Manuel's looks but also some of his moral confusions, his recklessness and obtuseness, and his capacity for unexpected magnanimity. Finally, in "The Story of the Fox-Brush," Manuel is reborn in Henry V as he overruns France with his ruffians and overwhelms the spirited Katharine of Valois with his gusto, impudence, idealism, and chicanery.

Chivalry also assesses the role of queens in implementing the idea of vicarship, in putting royal honor above mean and selfish ends, and in attending to the welfare of their realms and subjects in the same spirit that God attends to the welfare of mankind. In "The Story of the Sestina," Alianora realizes too late that she has not been true to these high imperatives of queenship in England. Seeing at first hand the plight of her subjects after years of civil war, and hearing the frank criticism of her old lover, Osmund Heleigh, who goes to his death to help her save her son—these experiences physic her pomp, bring wisdom to her later rule, and cause her to die a nun. In "The Story of the Choices," another foreign-born queen of England, Ysabeau—the victim of a marriage she had no part in making to the degenerate Edward II—falls to depths that Alianora never knew. Murder, promiscuity, and jealousy are among the evils that have defaced her honor. When she has one of her old lovers and his admirable lady "in domnei" completely in her vicious power, and would bring him down to her vileness by the choices she offers him, he surprises her by his self-sacrificial chivalry and even shocks her into an imitative gesture that partly redeems her in the reader's eyes.

Of all the foreign queens of England treated in *Chivalry*, the Dutch Philippa of "The Story of the Housewife" and the Bohemian Anne of "The Story of the Satraps" best understand the idea of vicarship that is one of the cornerstones of chivalry, but each queen interprets this idea in a different way. Philippa does not permit Edward III's mistress to upset her. When this mistress betrays him to the Scots while he is fighting in France and when the powerful barons of the realm show signs of following her in treachery, Philippa herself takes to the battlefield, and by such masculine chivalry shames the lukewarm and even the coldfooted to ardent patriotism. She thus turns seemingly certain defeat into stunning victory. At the same time she is a match for her ministers in statecraft, an attentive mother and wife, and a meticulous manager of all that pertains to the running of a household. She likes the chivalrous devotion of old John Copeland, her secretary, but is too sensible to let it distract her from her stewardship. Anne is more the saint than the administrator in her conception of the role of queen. Leaving affairs of state to the none-too-competent Richard II, she devotes herself to good works amongst the common people. She too has her servant "in domnei"—the cleric Edward Maudelain—but she will not sanction the ambitious utopian dream that tempts him when he discovers that he has a right to Richard's throne and powerful support to put him there. Anne's religious idealism, her abhorrence of war and contempt for political intrigue prevail upon him; and she remains faithful to the husband who does not deserve her.

The idea of woman-worship or domnei, with the kind of renunciation that accompanies it in *The Way of Ecben,* is stressed in *Chivalry.* Richard II becomes one of its exponents by a curious transformation of his character. The weakest story of the collection, "The Story of the Heritage," sets forth the improbable imposture that the quixotic Edward Maudelain carries out after he has fled to Wales and put behind him the dream of usurping the kingship of England. Bolingbroke, of course, does usurp it, imprisoning Richard II in the castle where Exton and his men later murder him. But Cabell tells us that by the agency of Horvendile—who appears here under the name of Orvendile—and by the cooperation of Richard's eleven-year-old second wife, Isabel of Valois, Maudelain is able to take Richard's place before the coming of the assassins. So in "The Story of the Scabbard" Richard finds himself miraculously free. He wanders about the world under the name of Richard Holland, joins Owain Glyndwyr (Owen Glendower) in Wales, and prepares a trap for Henry IV that is worthy of the similar traps set by Edward I in "The Story of the Rat-Trap" and Henry V in "The Story of the Fox-Brush." But meanwhile Richard falls chivalrously in love with the Welsh beauty, Branwen; and, for her sake, he decides, like Alfgar, to renounce his kingdom. So he lets Henry IV go, as Alfgar does Ulf. His scabbard has found in Branwen its permanent sheath.

"The Story of the Navarrese" plays a variation on the same theme. Antoine Riczi holds Jehane as his lady "in domnei." She must wed the old Duke of Brittany, but Riczi remains devoted to her, waiting for the Duke's death. When this eventually occurs, he goes to her—only to find that time and luxury have changed her. She commits the ultimate outrage against the code of domnei by commanding her faithful lover to serve as her proxy in a marriage to King Henry IV of England, whose power and wealth she covets. Even this gross offense on her part, however, fails to diminish the devotion of Riczi, who as the Vicomte de Montbrison comes as an ambassador to England. When her stepson, Henry V, has her taken into custody for witchcraft so he can confiscate her wealth, Riczi betrays his country to obtain her release. Although the death of Henry V restores her to her queenship as regent, she decides to renounce this supreme position for the man who, like another Perion, has cherished her so chivalrously over the years.

Perions likewise haunt *The Line of Love*. In "Adhelmar at Puysange," Adhelmar finds in Mélite a Melicent who thinks she really loves the man her brother has engaged her to marry—Hughes d'Arques. Adhelmar, though he has suffered an insult from d'Arques that customarily requires a duel to the death, rescues him from the law when he is jailed as a traitor. Then Adhelmar, mortally hurt in performing this generous exploit, comes back to Mélite—to die in the benison of her gratitude.

In "'Sweet Adelais,'" Fulke d'Arnaye—French prisoner of Hugh Vernon—regards Adelais Vernon, his captor's daughter, as his lady "in domnei," even though he knows that she is engaged to marry the Marquis of Falmouth. On the very day that Fulke is effecting a successful escape—with a boat awaiting him for the Channel crossing—he finds Roger Darke, Adelais' cousin, in the act of abducting her to force her into a marriage with him. Fulke rescues her from Darke and would forego his long-anticipated escape to take her safely home; but like another Melicent, she decides to forget her engagement to the Marquis of Falmouth and climbs in Fulke's boat, as his forever.

In "The Castle of Content," Will Summers—the supposedly bastard son of Tom Allonby—tells how he receives documentary proof of his legitimacy. With this proof he can have not only the estate and title now held by Stephen Allonby but also the Lady Adeliza—his own lady "in domnei"—to whom Stephen has been engaged. When he finds that the lady really loves Stephen, he helps them elope and uses the proof of his legitimacy to fire a bridge and thus foil their pursuers.

Though these three stories may show that the chivalrous tradition persisted into Renaissance times, they also suggest that one of its tenets—woman-worship or domnei—became a somewhat stereotyped masculine gesture of self-immolation.

V *The Rivet in Grandfather's Neck*

Such gesturing is certainly characteristic of Colonel Rudolph Musgrave, the protagonist of *The Rivet in Grandfather's Neck*, a romance-novel of Virginia from the 1890's to the 1920's, which is subtitled *A Comedy of Limitations* and is supposedly compiled by Richard Fentnor Harrowby, Lichfield's Nicolas de Caen. Musgrave's illegitimate half-brother, novelist John Charteris—who embodies both the gallant and the poetic attitudes toward life—thus ironically describes Colonel Musgrave: " 'No other man I know has ever attained the good old troubadourish ideal of domnei—that love which rather abhors than otherwise the notion of possessing its object.' "[9]

The Colonel's first gesture of self-immolation occurred sometime before the present action of *The Rivet* begins. After Anne Willoughby, his first love, married John Charteris, she might have got free from him had events taken their natural course. For Charteris committed adultery with Mrs. Pendomer, who bore him a son and then had to be divorced. If Anne had known, she would have had good grounds for divorcing Charteris. But to keep Anne happy in her marriage, Musgrave—who had formerly pursued Clarice Pendomer during the period when he was sowing his wild oats after the fashion of southern young men—pretended he was still her paramour, and made this white lie, or alabaster imposture, stick in Lichfield gossip.

The Colonel's second gesture of self-immolation is one of the *coups de théâtre* of the present action. Falling in love with Patricia Stapylton, his beautiful distant cousin who is over twenty years his junior, he feels safe from possessing her since she is engaged to an English earl. After thrashing the earl because of his unchivalrous treatment of Patricia, the Colonel finds that she is willing to be his. Their engagement is to be announced at a dinner party. Meanwhile the fickle Patricia takes a fancy to young Joe Parkinson. The Colonel then decides to sacrifice his own happiness to hers, as he had in the case of Anne. So at the dinner party he concludes one of his most eloquent orations by the altogether unexpected announcement of the Stapylton-Parkinson marriage.

On this occasion chivalrous self-immolation has on Patricia somewhat the same effect it had on Adelais Vernon in *The Line of Love*. When Patricia comes to tell the Colonel how distasteful she finds Joe Parkinson, the only thing the Colonel can do as a gentleman is to insist on marrying her forthwith before she changes her mind again. He now possesses the second object of his domnei and must make the most of it. Since he is still committed in the depths of his psyche to Anne Charteris, this marriage—even though it considerably improves his financial situation and though Patricia is surpassingly attractive physically—has its embarrassing side. But because the Colonel is the soul of honor, and because honor means to him what it meant to Dom Manuel—keeping up appearances and meeting one's obligations—he does his best to make this marriage a success.

From Patricia's point of view, it comes close to being a failure and, even though preserved, ends in tragedy. Daughter of an ex-overseer who made money in the North, she is an outsider to the chivalrous tradition the Colonel reveres and represents. Furthermore she has a shrewd intelligence. This combination permits her to see Musgrave with some objectivity. She remarks to his face: "'You are a fearful humbug in some ways, Rudolph.'" And she confides to John Charteris: "'Rudolph has all the virtues which a woman most admires until she attempts to live in the same house with them.'"[10]

Part of the humbug that annoys her is his rhetoric and mythmaking about the southern past. He regards the days before the Civil War as a kind of Golden Age, Lee and his gray battalions as Arthurian knights, the freeing of the slaves as a monstrous folly, and Reconstruction as an unmitigated evil perpetrated by the malice of carpetbaggers. His own title of "Colonel," however, is political or social rather than military in origin. Instead of doing anything that represents accomplishment in the domain of action, he is content to eke out a meager living as a professional genealogist concocting pedigrees for pseudo-aristocrats and as librarian and corresponding secretary for the Lichfield Historical Association. After marrying Patricia, he embellishes her ancestry so that she can move with pride in the best society, and at the same time he squanders her money on the stock exchange. After she has given him a son at the cost of shortening her own life, he spends almost as much time making speeches before patriotic and antiquarian organizations as he

devotes to her and the boy. He is a wholly impractical sentimentalist living in a world of words rather than actualities.

Among his "virtues" to which she scornfully refers, loyalty
is pre-eminent. He demonstrates it in his devotion to his sister
Agatha and in his refusal to consider discharging the mulatto
servant, Virginia. But it is a wholly uncritical loyalty that does
nothing about Agatha's dipsomania and declines to entertain
even a suspicion that Virginia does not live up to the image of
unswerving and loving fidelity that he has imposed upon her.
Knowing he is so uncritical in his loyalty, Patricia decides not to
tell him the truth about her physical condition—that in consequence of her inherited pelvic deformity, parturition, and too
much surgery, she has only so many months to live.

This awful knowledge is the justification for Patricia's desperate and immoral effort to snatch at happiness. Attracted to John
Charteris—as so many other women have been—she decides to
elope with him. Cognizant of their plans through eavesdropping,
the Colonel resorts to extreme measures to stop them. When his
revelation to Charteris that they are half-brothers fails, he wins
by appealing to Patricia's feelings as a mother and to her respect
for physical prowess. The irony of this melodramatic sentimentalism and violence is that it is motivated in large measure by
the desire to protect Anne Charteris from another scandal. The
Colonel's chivalry is indeed ambiguous in its decadence. But after
Charteris is murdered by another irate husband whose wife he
had not seduced, and Patricia has died on hearing the news,
the Colonel and Anne do not marry. Even when Anne knows
the whole truth about Charteris, she remains uncritically loyal
to his memory. And the Colonel matches this attitude, as his
rivet dictates.

The rivet in question invests him in the end with a little of
the dignity that Dom Manuel possessed. One of the Colonel's
favorite bits of reading is a fairy tale by Hans Christian Andersen
concerning an eloping china chimney-sweep and shepherdess and
a grandfather with a rivet in his neck that prevents him from
separating them afterwards. The Colonel interprets this simple
tale as a profound psychological and social allegory. "'There
is always the thing which one cannot do for the reason that
one is constituted as one is,'" he says. "'That, I take it, is the
real rivet in grandfather's neck and everybody else's.'"[11] His own
limitations as an inheritor of chivalrous traditions are his rivet.

And nowhere does he define this rivet more eloquently than when he says: " 'You cannot lead your own life, Patricia; none of us can. Each life is bound up with many others, and every rash act of yours, every hasty word of yours, must affect to some extent the lives of those who are nearest and most dear to you.' "[12]

This is the basis of his comedy, which—like Dom Manuel's in *Figures of Earth*—is also one of obligations. In living up to most of them, the Colonel becomes not altogether unworthy of comparison to his remote progenitor and also to King Alfgar of *The Way of Ecben*. Both comparisons come to mind at his moving death. He dies under the delusion that dead Patricia has come home again, that they are miraculously wafted to the Garden between Dawn and Sunrise, and that behind Patricia is the pool of Haranton and Manuel's unfinished clay figure of a man.

The use of the fairy tale about china people along with ingenious play on the word "rivet"; the sudden reversals and surprises; the stock minor characters; the resort to letters and eavesdropping to carry forward the action; the frequency of epigrammatic wit in the dialogue; the abrupt exit of characters seemingly at the whim of the puppet-master; the persistent, too obviously contrived ironies; the number of disgressive passages and speeches —these features of *The Rivet* give it occasionally a smack of the summer theater and a smell of the lamp.

The author is as guilty as his protagonist of being too much in love with rhetorical ornament. For example, he thus comments on Musgrave's morning conversation with Mrs. Pendomer at his house-party: "The Colonel was finding this matutinal talk to be discomfortably opulent in pauses."[13] The house-party is thus described: "People were assembling for supper, and passing to and fro under the low-hanging branches; and the gaily colored gowns of the women glimmered through a faint blue haze like that with which Boucher and Watteau and Fragonard loved to veil, and thereby to make wistful, somehow, the antics of those fine parroquet-like manikins who figure in their *fêtes galantes*."[14] The Colonel's repeated initial image of Patricia becomes a cloying refrain that has the unintentional effect of dissolving satire into sentimentalism: ". . . he had noted, for the first time, that her hair was like the reflection of a sunset in rippling waters, and that her mouth was an inconsiderable trifle, a scrap of sanguine curves, and that her eyes were purple glimpses of infinity."[15]

Perhaps the following critical observation from Cabell's *Some of Us* can be applied without too great injustice to Cabell himself: "When Maurice Hewlett dealt with contemporary life he advanced delicately between his deep-rooted sense of form and his glowing vocabulary, without ever touching either. This Hewlett, in brief, wrote balderdash mincingly, and was one of the over many disciples who have betrayed George Meredith."[16]

CHAPTER 4

The Way of Gallantry

I *Jurgen*

STUDENTS of the relationship between the short and longer forms of prose fiction should not neglect *Jurgen*. This extended romance evolved from a short tale entitled "Some Ladies and Jurgen" that Cabell wrote for *The Smart Set* in 1918.[1] In his Storisende Edition preface to *Jurgen*, he gave a slightly different account of the book's genesis, making it appear that the *Smart Set* story was merely a chip from the rough draft of the romance which was already half-written and completely planned. Burton Rascoe, by publishing a letter Cabell wrote him August 10, 1919, about the genesis of *Jurgen*, set right the true relation of the tale to the romance, as Cabell himself had to admit with humorously grudging apology in *Preface to the Past*.[2] The making of *Jurgen* was thus comparable to the making of Joyce's *Ulysses* and Mann's *The Magic Mountain*, both of which were originally conceived as short stories.

"Some Ladies and Jurgen" consists of the beginning and ending of *Jurgen* in its final version—with the exception of various minor changes and additions. The hero, a middle-aged poet, encounters a monk who is cursing the Devil for placing in the roadway a stone over which the monk has just tripped. Abridging some of his verses into prose, Jurgen impudently defends evil. Walking on, Jurgen meets a black gentleman who thanks him for his good word and hopes that his life will be free from care. When Jurgen ruefully implies that this is hardly possible since he is a married man, the stranger promises to reward him. Arriving home, Jurgen discovers that his wife, Dame Lisa, has mysteriously departed. Later, when she is seen behaving queerly near a cave beyond the town and tries to lead her relatives into the cave rather than heeding their injunctions to return home, Jurgen yields to family pressure and goes after her himself. Following her into the cave, he comes to the place where the black gentleman—who turns out to be more than the Prince of Darkness, since he is Koshchei the Deathless—is keeping accounts of the universe he has made and controls. When Jurgen indicates that he wants Lisa back, Koshchei evokes women whom he thinks much more suitable to be married to a poet. They are Queen Guenevere, Queen Anaïtis, and Queen Helen—standing for Faith, Desire, and Vision. Jurgen rejects each and still wants Lisa. So Koshchei produces her. She is her old self with a vengeance; she gives both Koshchei and Jurgen a tongue-lashing, and leaves for home. She is jealous of Jurgen and an old flame of his, Countess Varvara. After she has gone, Koshchei tries to persuade Jurgen to remain with him, but Jurgen insists that he must follow Lisa. He praises her as a poetess of domesticity, which time and habit have taught him to value above the faith, desire, and vision he no longer feels he can cope with. Shaking hands with Koshchei, he returns home to find Lisa as she was.

So much for the tale. It is noteworthy that the Jurgen it presents is primarily an aging poet rather than an exponent of the gallant attitude toward life. The theme is the compromise with conventional mores that poets make if they live long enough. Their wives may not understand them but none the less are indispensable to their comfort. The same theme is developed in the tale allocated to Miramon Lluagor in *The Silver Stallion.*

Cabell expanded "Some Ladies and Jurgen" into a full-length romance by sandwiching between the tale's beginning and ending the following episodes: (1) Jurgen's meeting with the Centaur (chapter II); (2) Jurgen's visit to the Garden between Dawn and Sunrise (chapters III-V); (3) Jurgen's visit to Mother Sereda (chapter VI); (4) Jurgen's recovery of a bygone Wednesday (chapter VII); (5) Jurgen's adventures in Glathion (chapters VIII-XX); (6) Jurgen's adventures in Cocaigne (chapters XXI-XXVI); (7) Jurgen's adventures in Leukê (chapters XXVII-XXXIII); (8) Jurgen in Hell (chapters XXXIV-XXXIX); (9) Jurgen in Heaven (chapters XL-XLII); and (10) Jurgen's re-encounter with Mother Sereda (chapter XLIII). The main purpose in the elaboration of all these episodes is to transform Jurgen from an old poet into a complete exemplar of the way of gallantry as Cabell understands it.

One of the origins of gallantry is the disillusionment that young men prone to chivalrous idealism experience in their youth when they accord domnei to women unworthy of it. To demonstrate this point with all the nuances that the perspective of maturity casts upon it is the purpose of two of the aforementioned episodes, the visit to the Garden between Dawn and Sunrise and the recovery of a lost Wednesday.

Jurgen's visit to the Garden between Dawn and Sunrise is a fantasy of what was but could not last. In this ideal place, for a whole summer, the young Jurgen loved Dom Manuel's blonde second daughter, Dorothy la Désirée—the Varvara of the tale. But the garden of their youthful illusion was destroyed by two repulsive allegorical creatures representing Bread and Butter. Dorothy married the wealthy Heitman Michael and began to take lovers. Jurgen found consolation for his broken heart in amorous promiscuity, married Lisa, and succeeded to the proprietorship of her putative father's pawnshop. The Countess Dorothy brings jewels to him occasionally to get money to pay for her lovers' gambling debts.

Jurgen's recovery of a bygone Wednesday is a fantasy of what might have come of this youthful affair had he acted more decisively. With all the knowledge he now has, he is back at that festive Wednesday at Storisende when the chivalrous Perion was falling in love with Melicent in *Domnei*. On the same occasion Heitman Michael was courting Dorothy. This time Jurgen kills his rival and embraces Dorothy as his own. But midnight comes. The bygone Wednesday is at an end. The Dorothy in his arms is the present aging, lust-worn countess, whom Jurgen finds so depressing a caricature of his first love that he puts her aside in a mood of gingerly virtue. Had the affair with Dorothy turned out otherwise and had he taken her as his wife, would the outcome have been vastly different? Would not the years have turned her anyway into something of what she has become? A corroding philosophical skepticism—the vivid sense of Time as the great ironist and destroyer—accompanies Jurgen's disillusionment with chivalrous love.

Gallantry requires an assumed mood of gayety—Hellenic in derivation—to cover its broken heart. Another of its requisites is the ability to see both sides of a question—one of the marks of the mature mind. And a third requisite is the kind of sexual vigor that youth alone insures. Only with these possessions can the gallant realize himself completely—in pragmatic exploration of experience, in avoidance of ideological commitment, and in giving women a full measure of physical pleasure. Jurgen's three favorite expressions—recurring as unifying motifs throughout his adventures—underscore these ends of gallantry: " 'I am willing to taste any drink once' "; " 'Of course you may be right; and certainly I cannot go so far as to say you are wrong: but still, at the same time—' "; and " 'I shall deal fairly with you.' "³

The episodes involving the Centaur and Mother Sereda—chapters II, VI, XLIII—dramatize Jurgen's equipment with all the requisites of gallantry. The Centaur Nessus—Hellenic to the hoofs—gives him the glittering shirt that he wears until he hands it over to Koshchei as ransom for Dame Lisa. This shirt is the gayety that is poison to the strong man and to the matter-of-fact man but a boon to the sensitive personality hurt by life or to the god who has had the misfortune to make things as they are. Mother Sereda, who has all Wednesdays or Time's middles in her care and who bleaches away whatever is colorful in existence, is also known as Aesred and Aderes—the three names being anagrams for Dea Res—the Thing Goddess. When she grants Jurgen that bygone Wednesday, she lets him keep his youthful body to accompany his middle-aged skeptical mind during his later adventures. Thus Jurgen is able to realize the ends of gallantry in a way that is unique.

In this incident and its consequences is one of the points of the subtitle—*A Comedy of Justice*. A great injustice of existence is that true intellectual maturity comes only after the diminishing of the physical powers, so that no man can fulfill his potentialities. Jurgen escapes this cruel irony—at least during the Walburga's Eve on which his adventures occur in Glathion, Cocaigne, Leukê, Hell, and Heaven. In the end, of course, he is anxious to give back his youthful body to Mother Sereda; for he knows that the mysterious shadow that has always accompanied him is her shadow—the shadow of Time's joy-killing wardress of the *via media*, the snooping, bleaching, commonsensical prude, Conformity and Respectability incarnate. He has fooled her by doing all his fair dealing in the dark out of the surveillance of her shadow. But this shadow has perpetually reminded him that his youthful vigor—with all the demands it makes on him—is but a loan. So the injustice of existence actually dogs him all along and catches up with him at last, even though Koshchei-Horvendile is most obliging and well-meaning. On the other hand, Jurgen breaks even, so to speak, by getting Dame Lisa back to administer to his creature comforts for at least a while longer.

In the course of Jurgen's five main adventures, mountebankery is a recurrent theme. He likes to refer to himself as " 'a monstrous clever fellow' "[4] and to cow his interlocutors with fraudulent erudition. He pretends in Glathion to be a duke, in Cocaigne a prince, in Leukê a king, in Hell an emperor, and in Heaven a pope. He is thus a kind of *picaro* who rises in society but is more interested in the fun of deception than in a room at the top.

Libertine sexuality is also a recurring theme in all these realms except Heaven. Jurgen possesses Guenevere illicitly before her marriage to Arthur or her affair with Lancelot. While participating in Glathion's knight-errantry, he seduces Yolande. Anaïtis surprises him more or less *in flagrante delicto* with his own stepgrandmother Sylvia and with one Stella, a yogini, " 'whatever that may be.' "[5] His marriage to Anaïtis in Cocaigne, to the hamadryad Chloris in Leukê, and to the vampire Florimel in Hell are prolonged experiments in phallic athleticism. His invasion of Queen Helen's privacy in Pseudopolis, the capital of Leukê, is indecorous and compromising, although without amorous results. Such results, however, are polyclimactic—so to speak —in his encounters with Queen Dolores of Philistia and Queen Phyllis of Hell.

Cabell's farcical handling of the themes of mountebankery and libertine sexuality distracts most readers' attention from the more serious implications of Jurgen's main adventures. But these serious implications are present, just as they are in Rabelais; and they lift the book immeasurably above the level of mere pornographic vaudeville. Jurgen's experiences in Glathion, Cocaigne, and Leukê are a skeptic's negative, pragmatic tests of great historical sytems of value or ways of life. His visits to Hell and Heaven, on the other hand, are this skeptic's more affirmative realizations of the roles played in human destiny by the dynamic illusions that pride and love engender.

Glathion and Cocaigne represent two complementary aspects of the medieval tradition—its Christian chivalry and its persistent pleasure-seeking, heretical paganism. The essence of Glathion's chivalry was "that all you possessed was loaned you to devote to the service of your God, your King and every woman who crossed your path."[6] The essence of Cocaigne's paganism was

" 'Do that which seems good to you' " and " '. . . the body of man is capable of much curious pleasure.' "[7] After finding out about some of the doings of the clergy, taking the measure of King Gogyrvan Gowr, and discovering in Guenevere "innocence combined . . . with a certain moral obtuseness,"[8] Jurgen rejects the chivalrous way and its value-system as irrational. After Jurgen has been initiated into all the rituals approved by Anaïtis—whose name is an anagram for "Insatia" with an erotic diaeresis—his verdict is "that all such employment" is "a peculiarly unimaginative pursuit of happiness" and that he certainly does not intend " 'to dwell eternally in a glorified brothel.' "[9]

Leukê represents the Hellenic tradition in both its conventional and its more creative phases. Modern culture—prefigured by Philistia with its realism and utilitarianism, its vulgar worship of novelty, phrases, and usage—is the enemy. Its victory over a merely sentimental or neo-classical decorum, from which Silenus escapes through drunkenness, does not strike him as serious. " 'Dullness will conquer dullness,' " he tells Jurgen, " 'and it will not matter.' "[10] But the supreme classical-romantic aestheticism embodied in Queen Helen and the city of Pseudopolis is something else. The reader's loyalties are intensely committed here, and he glories in the fact that Helen and her cohorts soar unharmed into the Empyrean and deride the Philistines and their devices. Submitting to these devices after declining the Queen of Philistia's generous offers, Jurgen is relegated to Limbo.

The hell that Jurgen visits is a creation of Koshchei to humor the pride of Jurgen's forefathers and his father—Coth of the Rocks—in their sins. Such arrogant consciences have these damned souls that, to meet their excessive demands for proper attention, the poor devils assigned to them are overworked to the point of exhaustion. The heaven that Jurgen visits is a creation of Koshchei to humor the notions of Jurgen's grandmother as shaped by her literal belief in the Bible and her immense capacity for unselfish love. Jurgen even encounters himself there, in all the perky angelhood of her indulgent fancying. The pride and love thus reflected are characteristically human rather than divine: indeed, they are precisely the emotions of which Koshchei is incapable.

The effect of both these episodes is to suggest another bearing of the subtitle—*A Comedy of Justice.* Perhaps—Cabell is telling the reader—there is a kind of ultimate justice, one so simple and so ironic that most of us have overlooked it. The dooms of men conform to the scope of their imaginings. They make their own hells and heavens. The blessed trouble about dreams is that they do someday come true.

Mother Sereda goes much beyond this speculation in her final reckoning with Jurgen: "'You jested with me. So I jest with you. Probably Koshchei jests with all of us. And he, no doubt,—even Koshchei who made things as they are,—is in turn the butt of some yet larger jest.'"[11]

As in *Figures of Earth* and *The Silver Stallion,* the topical satire dear to the anatomist shoots athwart the more universal comedy, especially in the Hell episode. "The religion of Hell is patriotism, and the government is an enlightened democracy." Observes Jurgen: "'I have long wondered who started the notion that the way to get a wise decision on any conceivable question was to submit it to a popular vote. Now I know!'" The war that Hell is waging against Heaven is referred to as "this interminable effort to make the universe safe for democracy. . . ."[12]

Most of the devices by which Cabell seeks to unify the obvious looseness of *Jurgen* have figured already in this discussion. But another device perhaps more calculated to insure magnitude than unity remains to be mentioned—the manipulation of six major myths. The Faust story is central—in Jurgen's befriending by the black gentleman and in his concern with Helen. In both the sexual and intellectual libertinism of Jurgen, Don Juan is reanimate. The Glathion episode levies on the Arthuriad; the Cocaigne episode, on Tannhäuser in the Venusberg. Jurgen's relationship to Dorothy la Désirée parallels that between Troilus and Cressida; his relationship to Dame Lisa, that between Ulysses and Penelope. The treatment of all six myths is comic, even parodic. The student of twentieth-century American fiction should contrast Faulkner's tragic use of myths in *Absalom, Absalom!,* where the House of David, the House of Atreus, and the House of Oedipus provide magnifying analogues for the House of Sutpen.

II *The Line of Love and The White Robe*

After *Jurgen,* with its Walburga's Eve occurring in 1277, Cabell's next major fiction concerning the gallant attitude is *The High Place,* whose action begins on a day in 1698. What of the gallant attitude between these dates? The answer is to be found in five tales representing different periods of Cabell's labors on the "Biography," and they do not afford a very consistent conspectus of his treatment of the theme.

"The Wedding Jest," written in 1919 and added to the revised *The Line of Love* of 1921, is the most definite of these short links between *Jurgen* and *The High Place* because its hero, Florian, Vicomte de Puysange, is reputed to be Jurgen's illegitimate son and is the chief fourteenth-century ancestor of the better-known protagonist of *The High Place,* who is also named Florian, fourth Duc de Puysange, Prince de Lisuarte, Marquis and Baron de Manneville, and Vicomte de Puysange. The first Florian is the Rip Van Winkle among Cabell's gallants.

On another Walburga's Eve, at precisely half an hour after his marriage to Adelaide de la Forêt, Florian absconds from the festivities to keep a rendezvous with the ghost of his dead comrade, Tiburce d'Arnaye, who had loved him more comprehendingly than any woman could. The three drinks they take together mark the passage of thirty years. When Florian returns to his bride on what he thinks is the morning after, he discovers that Adelaide—now a middle-aged widow playing chess with her old mother, Dame Melicent—has a grown daughter, Sylvie de Nointel, who resembles the Adelaide he married. Since he has kept his youth, there is no point in his professing that he still loves Adelaide. In fact, Time has transformed both Mama Adelaide and Grandmama Melicent into depressingly prosaic cynics. So he shifts his affections to the charming Sylvie, shrugs off the memory of earlier pledges, and is as happy as if Tiburce had never played him such a fantastic prank.

His gallantry emerges in his ability to compromise with the facts of life as he now finds them. The mood in which he turns to Sylvie must have been shared by many a man who came back from the rendezvous with death in World War I, saw that the world he had once been at home in was suddenly antiquated, and consoled himself with the new generation of "flaming youth." Awareness of Time as the great ironist and destroyer is here countered by the gayety, the resolute frivolity, that is one of gallantry's most effective gestures.

The White Robe: A Saint's Summary, completed in 1928 and incorporated as the third tale in the trilogy of *The Witch-Woman,* shows Dom Manuel's third daughter, Ettarre, misbehaving with a lover quite different from either Madoc the poet, or Alfgar the chivalrous king. This lover, Odo, is the wolf in sheep's clothing among Cabell's gallants.

More central to his story than his dealings with Ettarre is his relationship with the black magician, Gui de Puysange, one of the ancestors of the Florian of *The High Place*. When Odo is only a shepherd boy, Gui afflicts him with lycanthropy, so that he commits atrocities under the guise of a werewolf. Apprehended for his crimes, he finds that Gui is his judge. On the ground that he is insane rather than merely criminal, Gui has him committed to a monastery for therapy. Thinking that Gui is not the supreme master of evil that he pretends to be, Odo rises in the Church, becomes an abbot and eventually a bishop. Disbelieving in the Heaven he extols to his parishioners, he enjoys hearing about the sufferings of martyrs, delights in the torturing of heretics, commits further atrocities as a werewolf, succeeds in having Gui executed for a crime he himself has perpetrated, and wins an enviable reputation as a confessor of women. When he dies in his sleep, he finds himself on a magic carpet with the Ettarre he once loved but caused to be killed as a witch. She convinces him that he is on his way to the Heaven he has converted so many people to accept. When this possible outcome disturbs him, she explains that further misbehavior with her will damn him to her more pleasant Hades. He abstains, however, on the ground that he needs to help the victims of his Heaven. But after he enters this Heaven, he is in the hands of its overlord, his old master, Gui de Puysange.

The ironies of this weird tale, though manifold and sustained, are sometimes too obvious, too labored. The anticlericalism and the persistent emphasis on the ambiguity of good and evil are characteristic of Cabell in his most skeptical mood. The mountebankery of Odo is a fit subject for comedy, but not his penchant for committing sadistic atrocities on children. The comic tone Cabell assumes toward this penchant—while appropriate, perhaps, to a parody of the saint's legend as a literary form—horrifies rather than amuses. The tale, however, compels interest for its exploration of the connection between gallantry and diabolism— a connection stressed to some extent in *Jurgen* through Koshchei, Horvendile, and the Brown Man, and strikingly present in *The High Place*.

Three other tales of *The Line of Love* in its original version

emphasize the way of gallantry. "Love-Letters of Falstaff" brings
the now aged Sylvia Vernon—once Sylvia Darke—whom Sir John
loved forty years before in Norfolk and has not seen since, to
visit him at the Boar's Head Tavern. Drinking heavily and lying
often with Doll Tearsheet, he has been trying to forget his
recent humiliating rejection by Prince Hal, now King Henry V.
Sylvia, who has cherished Falstaff's memory all these years and
has heard only good things about him, leaves him the letters he
once wrote her. The experience of talking with her again and of
reading over these letters confronts him sadly with the Falstaff
that used to be and with the cruel trickery of Time. The reader
is reminded of Jurgen finding his way back to the Garden
between Dawn and Sunrise. But Sir John rallies the resources
of his sacked gallantry, laughs at the poetic-chivalrous rubbish
he scribbled in his youth, fills another cup to the brim, and for-
tifies himself for that night's bout with the lusty Doll Tearsheet.

In "The Conspiracy of Arnaye" the veteran gallant Raymond
d'Arnaye outfoxes the chivalrous fancies of his young niece
Matthiette so that she will fall in love with the husband he
wants her to take for political reasons—the gallant young Raoul
de Puysange, descendant of Jurgen and the first Florian. Puysange pretends to be one Raoul de Frison, Raymond's page, and
captures Matthiette's heart with his minstrelsy. When her uncle
insists on the Puysange marriage and the page bids her farewell,
she decides to risk all for love and joins him at his hut. Next
morning they are met by a troop of horsemen in honor of their
nuptials. The wise Raymond chuckles at his ruse of making
Puysange as attractive as forbidden fruit usually is.

Another conspiracy in accord with the conventions of love-
game comedy is the theme of "In Ursula's Garden." The present
Marquis of Falmouth once loved Kate Beaufort. But since she
was dowerless and he was just a cadet, he jilted her to
become a soldier of fortune. She vanished. Now that he has
risen in the world, he is vying for the hand of the wealthy Lady
Ursula with two other suitors—Master Richard Mervale and the
Earl of Pevensey. He is ready to fight the Earl for having
charmed Lady Ursula with libertine verse. Then he discovers
Mervale embracing her and is even more furious. His effort
to chastise Mervale results in the discovery that the latter is a
girl in disguise—the long-lost Kate. Apparently Kate and Ursula
—her relative—have conspired to trap the Marquis into this sit-

uation. Ursula is committed to the Earl and wants Kate to have her man. And the Marquis is now a pretty fair catch for a poor spinster! Kate succeeds—but in the shrewd spirit of the female gallant bringing a slightly obtuse, none-too-faithful or chivalrous "good soldier" to the matrimony that he whilom evaded to his professed nostalgic regret. Traces of Melicent and Perion survive, but in a lighter, more casual world.

III *The High Place*

It is difficult to generalize about the protagonist of *The High Place*, a major romance, because of the dream devices Cabell employs. The ten-year-old boy Florian, descended from Jurgen and the Florian of "The Wedding Jest," goes to sleep one day in 1698 in his father's garden at Storisende after having read the fairy tales of Perrault and stared too long at the distant forest of Acaire. He dreams that he enters the forest and finds Princess Melior, the sleeping beauty, held in enchantment on the high place since medieval times. Presumably awakened by his father, he grows to manhood, lives according to the decadent gallant code of the Orléans regency in the early eighteenth century, but —before making his fifth marriage—becomes involved with the sleeping princess of his childhood dream. This involvement is the substance of his story. It is a story about to end in disaster when he really wakes up to discover that he has been dreaming all along. Then an epilogue informs us that he later lives his actual life pretty much as he dreamed it, with the important exception that he avoids any entanglement with Melior, marries instead the fifth wife he had originally intended to marry, and goes graveward conforming to the Regency code.

Did Florian succeed or fail as an exponent of gallantry? The answer differs according to which Florian the reader is talking about. The Florian of the long dream is an apostate to gallantry by reason of his attempt to realize poetic and chivalrous ideals regardless of the costs—and they are heavy. The Florian of actuality learns a lesson from his dream, prudently declines to be taken in by the notion of making poetic and chivalrous ideals come true, and remains to the end a successful, albeit a decadent gallant.

Most critics of this book have deplored the dream device as hackneyed and as serving no useful purpose. Cabell apparently found it necessary to force the reader to contemplate from a novel point of view the beauty celebrated by poets and the holiness iconized by the code of chivalry. This novel point of view may be defined as that of decadent gallantry in league with diabolism, for the decadence of Florian's gallantry is beyond question. He has been brought up not to offend the notions of his neighbors. He professes great respect for precedent. His sense of honor prevents him from ever being false to his given word. Yet he has seduced innumerable women and murdered four wives. Preparing to marry a fifth, he must make way for her by poisoning the boy he has been keeping as a "mistress." In short, he is a bisexual Bluebeard behind a hypocrite's mask.

To restore the enchanted past of the high place to wide-a-wake life, Florian enters with the mysterious Brown Man, Janicot, into a pact that entails monstrous crimes. This Pan-figure has outlived many gods and so is biding his time until his adversaries in the Christian Heaven pass. Meanwhile he and the Archangel Michael, when occasion warrants, enjoy drinking together and exchanging philosophical reflections. Janicot's black magic can cause the departed and the immortal to appear without warning. Once, however, when he calls up Horvendile, Janicot himself vanishes. This Janicot-Horvendile takes a naturally fiendish delight in enabling Florian to discover that neither the beauty of his dream-princess, Melior, nor the holiness of his patron saint, Hoprig, is quite what—since childhood—he has assumed each to be. The subtitle, then—*A Comedy of Disenchantment*—has both a literal and a figurative meaning.

Melior, released in Florian's long dream from her centuries-old spell and taking the place of his intended fifth wife, retains her superlative, but wholly physical beauty. Spiritually, she is null; intellectually, she is a void. But the most intolerable of her defects is a platitudinous and none-too-coherent garrulity about the inconsequential. Florian soon finds his dream-princess such a bore that he anxiously looks forward to her passing, as specified in his pact with Janicot; he cannot face the possibility of an extension of her stay. The last blow is the knowledge that the child she bears him is not his but his patron saint's. His enchanted bride was "damaged goods," to borrow the English title of Brieux's famous play. Hoprig—as Truewit of Ben Jonson's *Epicoene* would have expressed it—had antedated Florian cuckold.

For Hoprig, to whom Florian has so long addressed his prayers, is a saint by error. When the Church canonized an early Christian martyr by the name of Horrig, the weather had worn away the tail of the first *R* in his name on his gravestone, with the result that he was officially called Hoprig. The real Hoprig was a pagan high-priest and persecutor of Christians. He had, indeed, been responsible for Horrig's martyrdom. All this time Hoprig has been on the high place instead of attending to Florian's prayers. As a result of the Church's action, a permanent halo appears over his head. Active again, he finds this halo something of a nuisance, especially during nocturnal escapades, but he has to live with it as best he can. His way of discharging his new duties makes him a celestial problem case. He is the original of that figure which R. W. B. Lewis in *The Picaresque Saint* finds so ubiquitous in the modern novel.

Florian's long dream has a definite plot arising out of the consequences of his failure to marry his intended fifth wife and out of his efforts to live up to each item in his pact with Janicot. Cabell felt that this plot—which includes two murders and a visit to Antan in company with Horvendile for the purpose of obtaining the magic sword Flamberge—gave *The High Place* a unity of action lacking in his other full-length romances.[13] His view is to some extent justified, but the fact remains that this plot necessitates scenes of sophistication, depravity, and crime beyond the scope of a ten-year-old's dreaming, even though the boy is unusually precocious and the period is unprecedentedly corrupt. Hence, what is gained in unity is lost in convincingness.

The fact also remains that some of the most memorable writing is slightly extraneous to the development of the plot. In the chapter entitled "The Armory of Antan," the critic must consider, for example, the anatomy of man's destructiveness as well as the extreme pessimism flaunted by Florian as he practices sophistry on Queen Freydis to obtain Flamberge. He eventually obtains it through his amorous prowess rather than his sophistry, but Cabell spins out the latter to include such observations as the following: "What dignity was possible in an arena we entered in the manner of urine and left in the shape of ordure?"[14]

Beauty and holiness are potent illusions with which the way of gallantry—to be successful—should avoid having too intimate traffic. The main difference between the Jurgen of the Wal-

burga's Eve adventures and the Florian of the long dream is
that Jurgen has sense enough to leave Queen Helen undisturbed
when he finds her sleeping in Pseudopolis and to depart hastily
from the Heaven of his grandmother "without having gained or
wasted any love there,"[15] whereas Florian carries too far the
pragmatic test in his dealings with the high place. Since gallantry
is the way of the world, it should leave unto high places the
things that are theirs and not try to loose them into ordinary
living with the aid of diabolism, which has a tendency toward
extremes. The moral lesson that the Florian of the long dream
presumably transmits, then, to the actual Florian is simply the
classic one of moderation. He has learned it the hard way.

The role of dialectic and counterpoint in the "Biography" is
richly apparent as we put *Figures of Earth* alongside *Jurgen*.
Manuel tests gallantry and finds it lacking in his affair with
Alianora; Jurgen tests chivalry and finds it lacking in his affair
with Guenevere. Manuel tries to live up to his obligations and
confronts death with dignity; Jurgen evades the supreme commitments and accepts compromise with a shrug. Equally apparent is Cabell's reversal of positions as we move from *Domnei* to
The High Place. The gallantry of Demetrios and the diabolism of
Ahasuerus are the comic butts of Platonic-Christian idealism. The
Platonic-Christian ideals represented by Melior's beauty and
Hoprig's holiness become instruments of diabolic burlesque to
make clear that gallantry should stick to the middle marches
and the lowlands.

IV *Gallantry*

Gallantry, a collection of ten tales with a fictional "afterpiece"
in addition to "the epistle dedicatory," and a verse prologue
and epilogue, enhances the counterpoint and dialectic of the
"Biography." For it serves its theme—the gallant attitude—in the
same way that *Chivalry* does the chivalrous attitude. Like that
volume, it represents Cabell's earlier phase, is highly conventional in its technique, and attempts to recapture the atmosphere
of a definite historical period. The conventions followed, for
the most part, are those of eighteenth-century comedies of manners and intrigue; the prime emphasis is on the love-game and
there is some treatment of the game of politics. The period is
the very middle of the eighteenth century, with the action of
nine of the stories occurring in 1750 from March into September.

The tenth story and the afterpiece belong to the autumn of 1755. The settings include Usk, Tunbridge Wells, the Continent—both Poictesme and elsewhere—and two English country estates.[16]

The unity and the overall design are more impressive than in *Chivalry*. The reader's attention is on four couples who with other partners move successively across the stage like figures in some mazy dance—half antic hay, half minuet. A fifth male involved with several women partners emerges as the final, central figure; through his movements the spirit of the dance finds its most ironic expression and through his eyes the reader gains perspective on the other dancers. Another male figure—murdered while the dance is in progress—tantalizes the imagination; but he is too minor and underdeveloped to count for much in the interpretation of the dance's ultimate meaning.

The first couple is an older fop, George Erwyn, and an aging coquette, Anastasia Allonby—rich, pleasure-loving, and a widow. In "Simon's Hour," the reader gains some sense of Lady Allonby's power over men—both through her wealth and her vestigial voluptuousness—when the unscrupulous Lord Rokesle tries to force her to marry him and when her old admirer, Simon Orts (Lord Rokesle's lackey-and-pander cleric) saves her at the cost of his own life in a burst of recessive, half-cynical chivalry. In "Love at Martinmas," Lady Allonby wins the husband she wants in Mr. Erwyn. She had feared that her rival was her own stepdaughter, Dorothy, and the fear was well-grounded insofar as Mr. Erwyn was concerned. But Dorothy, who cleverly evades the ardor of Mr. Erwyn, turns his attempt at a proposal into a declaration in favor of her stepmother.

The second couple is Captain Audaine and Dorothy Allonby. The Captain is a bluff, pompous, hearty fellow; Dorothy is a dashing, aggressive, fashionable "roaring girl." Whereas all the other tales in *Gallantry* are told in the third person by the omniscient author, "The Casual Honeymoon" and "The Rhyme to Porringer" are first-person narratives in the Captain's own inimitable inflated prose. In the former tale he elopes with Dorothy's grandmother by mistake and thinks he is married to her, but the parson performing the ceremony is discovered to be a fraud. In the other story, the Captain plays the role of burglar to foil an anti-Jacobite agent and thus accidentally becomes Dorothy's rescuer from a forced marriage as repellent to her as the one planned for her stepmother by Lord Rokesle was to the intended victim. Finally, in "Actors All," Dorothy—by disguising as a man, by fencing skillfully, by lying adroitly, and by exploiting masculine psychology unscrupulously—saves the Captain from being executed for treason at the behest of the great anti-Jacobite, the Duke of Ormskirk.

The third couple is the Duke of Ormskirk and Claire de Puysange. Ormskirk or John Bulmer is in the mid-forties and is eminent both in amour and power politics. More importantly he is an amateur skeptical philosopher who wittily plays with ideas as well as with empires and morals. His complex gallantry, like Jurgen's, hides a frustrated youthful chivalry. He lost his Alison to Lord Brudenel and is now betrothed to Alison's daughter, Marian. When in "April's Message" he discovers that Marian is really in love with young Lord Degge—his own hireling—Ormskirk refuses to interfere, keeps Lord Brudenel from interfering, and relinquishes Marian to Degge out of a magnanimity inspired by his broken heart of long ago. "In the Second April" tells how, using his name John Bulmer, Ormskirk courts in Poictesme the young Claire de Puysange under the pretense that he is Ormskirk's representative. His courtship recaptures the chivalry of his youth, although he accomplishes his deeds of derring-do against the bandit Achille Cazaio with a banter more waggish than heroic. Both Claire and the wily Louis de Soyecourt—the second in command to Claire's brother Gaston, Duc de Puysange—are cognizant of Ormskirk's identity from the beginning. Had Gaston not returned in the nick of time, Ormskirk—through his nostalgic chivalrous folly—might have gone to his grave rather than to Claire's bridal bed.

The fourth couple is Gaston de Puysange and his Duchess Hélène. Hélène has cuckolded him with the aid of Louis de Soyecourt. But in "Heart of Gold" when Gaston discovers their intimacy, Hélène turns his jealousy into renewed fidelity by her clever acting and with a locket to which he attaches the same significance that Othello did to Desdemona's handkerchief.

In "The Scapegoats" and "The Ducal Audience," Louis de Soyecourt serves to throw into vivid relief the clash between amour and power politics that marked this period in the history of gallantry. In reaction against his father, the old Prince de Gâtinais—who holds the chivalrous view that all should be sacrified for God and France—Louis refuses to make a political marriage, disguises as a piano tuner, and lives happily and selfishly with his mistress, Nelchen Thorn, an innkeeper's daughter. The old Prince finds him out, poisons Nelchen, kills his own tool-villain valet, and then commits suicide—all to make sure the gallant Louis will turn chivalrous and fulfill his political destiny.

Given so melodramatic a push, Louis goes through with the Prince's wishes that he marry Victoria von Uhm and rule in Noumaria to strengthen France's position on the Continent. Gallantry soon sways Louis, however, and he is having an affair with a baroness. Then the baroness jilts him for the Comte de Chateauroux, and Louis' Duchess participates in the trick that leads him to hand over his mistress to his rival. But, in doing so, the Duchess convinces him that she is clever enough to rule in Noumaria in his stead. So he is off again, in his old guise of a piano tuner, to follow the way of gallantry.

In the afterpiece—"Love's Alumni"—he visits Ormskirk's estate in Westmorland, where a party is in progress, meets the four main couples previously discussed—as well as Degge and his Marian of "April's Message"—and finds them all reasonably happy after five years of marriage. "These people," Louis reflects, "made no pretensions to immaculateness; instead, they kept their gallant compromise with imperfection. . . ."[17]

Curiously enough, diabolism almost got into *Gallantry* as it gets into *Jurgen, The White Robe,* and *The High Place.* It appears embryonically in Simon Orts's brother Frank—an actor whose stage name is Francis Vanringham. In "The Casual Honeymoon" this Vanringham had planned to carry off Dorothy Allonby's old grandmother and to blackmail her with a fake marriage. In "The Rhyme to Porringer," he serves as Captain Audaine's emissary and confederate in the Jacobite conspiracy. In "Actors All," Vanringham turns "King's evidence" for Ormskirk and is one of the opponents whom Dorothy must outmaneuver to save her lover. In "The Scapegoats," the ex-actor is the old Prince de Gâtinais' tool-villain valet, stabbed to death by his master for the sake of Louis de Soyecourt's future. In retrospect, Cabell took more interest in this shadowy red-haired scoundrel than in all the other characters; he perceived in him the germ of Horvendile that failed to spawn.[18]

Despite the structural superiority of *Gallantry* to *Chivalry* and to *The Line of Love* as an ingeniously interrelated sequence of tales, the book has serious limitations in the treatment of its theme and in the quality of its comedy. The gallant attitude—

except for some of Ormskirk's incidental reflections—lacks the philosophical dimensions it assumes in such maturer fictions as *Jurgen, The High Place,* and even *The White Robe.* The comedy, instead of being cosmic, is social in the lighter sense. Intrigue, farce, and manners for their own superficial sakes predominate over the critical spirit that characterizes Cabell at his best. Cabell's apology is that *Gallantry* "is everywhere a book of beginnings."[19] But the fact remains that, in the larger design of the "Biography," it is not intended to introduce its theme but to expand and develop it. And this is precisely what it so cleverly and so artificially falls short of doing.

V *The Cords of Vanity and Its Appendices*

Treating the way of gallantry in the Virginia of Cabell's youth —from 1884 to 1903—*The Cords of Vanity,* a long fiction, parallels *The Rivet in Grandfather's Neck* in the series devoted to the way of chivalry. The hero of *The Cords of Vanity,* Robert Etheridge Townsend, born 1877, is a younger contemporary of the hero of *The Rivet,* Rudolph Vartrey Musgrave, born in 1856. John Charteris, the novelist spokesman of *Beyond Life,* plays a minor—but not unimportant—role in *The Cords,* as he does in *The Rivet;* his murder for an adultery he did not commit provides a bit of ironic melodrama for the endings of both stories.

Each title suggests that the attitude exemplified in the hero is a bias of tradition or heritage that limits the full human development of his personality. Musgrave is somewhat inflexible in his self-immolating idealism; Townsend is bound by his egoistic avoidance of full moral responsibility in his dealings with others. The critical spirit that is to some extent held in abeyance in *Gallantry* has in *The Cords* a less restricted tether. Townsend, a descendant of Ormskirk and Claire, exposes their sentimental worldliness in a milieu where its charm looks alternately callow and callous. The subtitle—*A Comedy of Shirking*—suggests such a perspective. But as in *Gallantry,* the comedy is that of the earlier Cabell; it is more social than cosmic, with the philosophic resonances not fully sounded.

Among the longer fictions of the "Biography," *The Cords* can lay claim to two distinctions, one invidious and the other dubious. The first is that it has been the most generally and perennially disliked by Cabell's critics, largely because of its hero's moral weaknesses. The second is that it is the only one written in the first person of the protagonist—a focus that Cabell experiments with in one tale of *The Line of Love*, "The Castle of Content"; in two tales of *Gallantry*, "The Casual Honeymoon" and "The Rhyme to Porringer"; and in the tale "Concerning David Jogram," found in the "Biography's" last volume of odds and ends. Curiously enough, Cabell wrote the first draft of *The Cords* entirely in the third person—which persists vestigially in all the chapter-headings—and then recast it into Townsend's own story. This change veils the critical spirit in an irony that would be more effective were it more pervasive and consistent. The consequence is that in *The Cords* the form of the confession dominates novel, romance, and anatomy in a way not to be matched elsewhere in the "Biography." This fact has led many of Cabell's critics into the error of regarding *The Cords* as a kind of fictional autobiography. Although Cabell has here levied on the Rockbridge Alum, Williamsburg, and Richmond, and perhaps recalled a number of his early philanderings in these and other places, this material—as in all his other fictions—has been transmuted and should not be identified with the data of his own life any more literally than much that occurs in *Jurgen* or *The Rivet* or *The Cream of the Jest*.

The many women in Townsend's saga have little of the allegorical significance of several of those in Jurgen's. Rather, they are types that may be placed in three main categories—the good women whom he truly loves, the more pliant ones whom he can never respect under the double standard of morality, and the miscellaneous in-betweens whom he courts with more or less sincerity but comes a cropper with for one reason or another. His involvements with these types constitute the substance of his story.

The good women whom he truly loves are two—his first love, Stella Musgrave, and his college friend, Bettie Hamlyn, daughter of his Latin professor. Because Stella desires to be the shaper of a successful man of the world, she marries Peter Blagden, who has inherited even more wealth than she has and who in her eyes has a future in law and politics if he can be kept away from the bottle. Townsend, even when she is dying after an accident, confirms her in this illusion as well as in the hope that she will survive. As the years pass following her death, he cherishes her memory as she really was, while she is becoming a legend seldom and dimly recalled by others, including her husband. She is to Townsend what Alison is to Ormskirk in *Gallantry*. As for Bettie, Townsend always thinks of her as more of an intelligent and wittily critical confidante than as an object of chivalrous devotion. He keeps her informed about his travels, his writings, and his amours largely through letters. Only when time and frustration have taught him the need for her mothering does he turn to her to find the wife he has mistakenly sought elsewhere. The affection that these two admirable women somewhat unaccountably entertain for Townsend redeems him slightly for the reader. Had either ever known the full truth about him, however, it is doubtful her affection would have lasted.

Much of this truth in all its ultimate caddishness is exhibited in his relations with the pliant women for whom he cannot retain respect. The former Amelia Van Orden—an outcast from his own world who married the unscrupulous Lethbury, became the actress Alys Montmorenci, and shines on the concert stage as Nadine Neroni, protégée of the Baron von Anspach—helps initiate Townsend to gallantry, but he can only pity her. Another unsatisfied married woman, Gillian Hardress, turns him into a seasoned adulterer. In the end he rejects her with inhuman candor. She makes him feel that he has been guilty of three deaths: that of the illegitimate child she bore him; that of Charteris, whom Hardress shot under the mistaken belief he was the child's father; and that of Hardress himself, who took his own life after this crime of insane jealousy. With reference to several other pliant women encountered in Europe, Townsend suppresses the details; but the reader knows that he seduced and abandoned one Agnès Faroy and that his role in her unhappy destiny sounds wholly indefensible.

The miscellaneous women of the third category figure in the more amusing episodes. After saving the mysterious Elena Barry-Smith from a burning hotel in Liège and likening her to Helen of Troy, Townsend discovers that widow Elena is from a vulgarly provincial family of the American South. She spiritedly rejects him for his snobbishness and for his insulting reference to her frailty on one occasion in their courtship. When he courts Marian Winwood at a Virginia summer resort with the ulterior motive of getting first-hand material for a novel, he is chagrined to find that she had the same motive and has beaten him into print with all his choicest scenes. Becoming betrothed to Rosalind Jemmett, heiress of a fruit-extract family, Townsend—whose own father had married into a baking-powder family—breaks the match off when he realizes that she deserves a solid-citizen Orlando rather than an arty Jaques like him. He courts Avis Beechinor—poor relation of the heiress Margaret Hugonin—under the illusion that she is really Margaret herself. He has based this belief on the evidence of a handkerchief in Avis' possession with Margaret's initials on it. When he first met Avis, he dropped a cigarette case he had borrowed from his host, the wealthy widower, Peter Bladgen. Misled by the initials thereon, Avis thinks he is Peter pretending to be Townsend and encourages his advances. Avis' mother eventually sees to it that this double misadventure in fortune-hunting ends more happily for her Avis.

These episodes, although amusing enough, detract considerably from Townsend's stature as an exemplar of gallantry. They also date *The Cords* as belonging to the era of Anthony Hope, Frank Stockton, and O. Henry. The flavor of Oscar Wilde's *The Picture of Dorian Gray*—caught early in the story in the discipleship of the as yet naïve Townsend to the sophisticated, even diabolic Charteris, who talks in the vein of Lord Henry Wotton—adds to this impression that *The Cords* is too much of an antiquated period piece to serve as a fitting completion of the theme first fully developed in the design of the "Biography" by *Jurgen.*

One of the faults of the far greater *Jurgen*—episodic looseness of structure—is also the most serious defect of this apprentice work. Cabell originally labelled *The Cords* "a picaresque romance of hedonism,"[20] thereby signifying his awareness of its rambling movement from one pursuit of pleasure, one exhibition of selfishness, to the next. The devices he has employed to unify it—the prologue "Fable of the Foolish Prince," the manipulation of Charteris and Bettie Hamlyn, the later re-entry of other characters introduced earlier—fail to give the action a close weave, an inevitable pattern, or a convincing logic. Nor do they dissipate the growing tedium of its unnecessary prolixity. Townsend develops from innocence to what he takes to be sophistication, but his double failure in the end to face up either to Hardress or to Bettie leaves the reader with the conviction that his extended sentimental education has resulted in nothing more than con-

The Way of Gallantry

temptible, equivocating cowardice. This conviction scarcely accords with what Cabell has been trying to tell the reader from the outset of the "Biography" about the virtues of the way of gallantry. Rather, it must be regarded as the unintended *non sequitur* of an immature Casanova's fumbling account of himself.

The volume following *The Cords* in the Storisende Edition presents Cabell's collected verse, *From the Hidden Way*, as one of Townsend's several published works. Bound up with it is Cabell's only play, *The Jewel Merchants*, a dramatization of one of the tales of *The Certain Hour*. "This play," Cabell remarks cryptically, "speaks with decision the last word as to gallantry, and as to what gallantry becomes when it is uninhibited; for the Duke is but Townsend freed from every nature of restraint."[21] Both the poems and the play thus presumably serve as appendices to *The Cords* and as a kind of coda on the way of gallantry as a theme.

So viewed, they leave us with a somewhat ambiguous image of Townsend and of gallantry's ultimate value. The poet of *From the Hidden Way* is interested in such beautiful women of legendry and literature as Helen in "False Dawn in Troy," Faustina in "Marcus Aurelius: A Suppressed 'Meditation,'" the Hörselberg Aphrodite in "Dame Venus in Thuringia," Shakespeare's Juliet and Cressida in "Jaunts from Stratford," and Congreve's Millamant in "'The Way of the World,'" to name but a few. Oppressed by the power of Death and Time, as in "The God-Father," he confronts them and their coadjutors with the gay challenge of "Invitation to the Voyage." He uses springtime, the philosophers, and *carpe diem* to obtain a kiss, as in "'—But Wisdom is Justified of Her Children,'" and renounces the ocean to lie and dream on the sandy shore behind a hillock, as in "Sea-Scapes."

Some of these verses are presented as adaptations from the work of the Duke Alessandro de Medici, who personifies bestial lust in *The Jewel Merchants* and whose two most memorable speeches are: "It is not possible to draw inspiration from a woman's beauty unless you comprehend how easy it would be to murder her"—and "Now, if I kill you, it is always diverting to kill; and if by any chance you should kill me, I shall at least be rid of the intolerable knowledge that to-morrow will be just like to-day."[22] Which face of gallantry is the reader finally to accept? Is its jaunty urbanity a mask for a darker degeneracy, its Hellenic this-worldliness inseparable from diabolism?

CHAPTER 5

The Way of Poetry

I *The Music from Behind the Moon and The Line of Love*

AS HAS BEEN SHOWN, Cabell does not permit the reader to forget the importance of the poetic attitude even when his main concern is the delineation of chivalry or gallantry. The poet's creative urge was strong in Dom Manuel; Jurgen, as a middle-aged pawnbroker, still composed verses; Miramon Lluagor as a magician was actually a prototype of the married poet and his problems. Both Charteris and Townsend were successful writers, and Duke Alessandro de Medici of *The Jewel Merchants* was a lyricist as well as a beast. And always Horvendile, fading in and out, has played God after the fashion of a devil and a poet. Fiction concentrating on exponents of the poetic attitude does not occur in the "Biography," however, until *The Music from Behind the Moon* and the two stories of *The Line of Love*—"In Necessity's Mortar" and "Porcelain Cups." Their purpose is to dramatize motifs that Cabell considers central to his understanding of the way of poetry, as defined in both *Beyond Life* and *Straws and Prayer-Books*.

Like its companion pieces—*The Way of Ecben* and *The White Robe*—*The Music from Behind the Moon* follows the pattern of a pilgrimage or a life's summary. But its divisions are shorter and more numerous, and its prose is more consistently cadenced and has more heightened diction. The result is a form admirably suited to the theme—a kind of prose poem.

The first part, "Of Madoc in His Youth," portrays a minor poet whose intimations and vision of ideal beauty leave him dissatisfied with all his creative efforts. When the reader meets him, he is a mere apprentice among court poets. His king and other connoisseurs disparage his art, although the ladies like his looks. He himself knows that his songs do not succeed in capturing an exotic music that keeps haunting him. Ettarre appears to him, revealing the source of this music. He tries to escape its strains by singing patriotic and sensually optimistic songs. These bring him applause but no release from his obsession.

The second part, "Of Madoc in This World," shows the successful but inwardly desperate poet seeking to find Ettarre at all costs, so that he can destroy her distracting music. He becomes internationally famous as a poet of peace, philanthropy, and other utilitarian and didactic themes, but that music of Ettarre makes all his achievements smack of impermanent silliness. Finally, he frightens Maya of the Fair Breasts into divulging the direction to the Waste Beyond the Moon, where Ettarre is held in supernatural durance; Maya had desired to turn him into one of her domesticated animals on Mispec Moor—the anagrammatic place of Compromise.

The third part, "Of Madoc in the Moon," narrates the poet's rescue of Ettarre from this durance. He reaches her on a hippogriffin that should be almost as famous a symbol in American literature as Hawthorne's scarlet letter, Melville's white whale, and Crane's blue hotel. "Upon the breast of the hippogriffin grew red plumage, its back was of a dark blue color, and its wings were white."[1] Having found Ettarre, Madoc forgets his intention to destroy her, embraces her with passionate love, and, by boldly adding a decimal point to the term of her bondage as recorded in the Book of the Norns, makes it possible to bring her back to earth immediately on his glittering, tricolored hippogriffin. His revision of the Book of the Norns, it should be noted, is "an exercise in arithmetic rather than in aesthetics"—to quote Cabell's remark in *Some of Us* on his own achievement in the "Biography." Furthermore, this revision decisively abolishes 584 years of earth's history, as the Norns had decreed it. These three weird literary sisters agree laughingly in "their quiet studio, by Yggdrasill" that they can't control the poets they have put into their vast epic. Says Verdandi: " 'Oh, yes, I see! . . . it is a poet altering the history of Earth.' " Chimes Urdhr: " 'These poets! they are always trying to escape their allotted doom.' " Caps Skuld: " 'One almost pities them at times.' "[2]

The fourth part, "Of Madoc in the Old Time," depicts the ironic destiny of all aging poets who have possessed ideal beauty and sought to turn it into an earthly figure. Splendor and ease and fame are Madoc's, but he seldom composes new songs, and Ettarre has to give so much attention to her children and other domestic problems that she can no longer strike from her heart-strings the music that was not of this world. Only at her funeral pyre, while white-robed boys are singing Madoc's great hymn concerning immortality, does her music skirl again inside the distraught skull of Madoc, provoking him to sudden inappropriate loud laughter. Becoming a slightly deranged but always happy vagabond, he follows after that music down the labyrinthine ways the rest of his old life.

More concisely and drastically than any of Cabell's other fictions about poets, *The Music from Behind the Moon* defines the end of poetry's quest as the supernal beauty described by Poe in "The Poetic Principle." Like Shelley's *Alastor* and Keats's *Endymion*, it conceives this quest as the lifelong pursuit of an elusive perfection. Like Poe's "Israfel" and Rossetti's "The Blessed Damozel," it emphasizes the chasm that divides the realm of essence from the realm of matter.

"In Necessity's Mortar" is one of the stories that appeared in the original version of *The Line of Love*. Its theme is the peculiar economy by which the poet is paradoxically destined to live in order that he may triumph over fate by creating something it cannot destroy so easily as it destroys him. This is an economy of living to the hilt, in disregard of personal waste and loss, for the sake of one's art and its lasting values. The love story of François Villon and Catherine de Vaucelles serves as vehicle. As one of the Companions of the Cockleshell, Villon has soiled and dissipated himself in murder, thievery, lechery, and drunkenness; but out of such experiences he has made his poems. He throws away the chance of winning back Catherine, the one woman he has really loved; but he uses the three wishes with which he takes leave of her as the motifs of a new ballade. Some such image of the poet as a supremely thrifty spendthrift, Dylan Thomas has made vivid in this present epoch.

Cabell wrote "Porcelain Cups" in 1919 and added it to the revised *The Line of Love* of 1921. He designed it to restate the theme of "In Necessity's Mortar" and, at the same time, to go considerably further in defining the poetic attitude. It does so by bringing this attitude into the sharpest possible contrast with its rivals—the chivalrous and the gallant attitudes. Although the way of gallantry, flaunting its casual, worldly insensitivity to the dedications of both chivalry and poetry, carries the broad Elizabethan day that is the tale's setting, its triumph does not

extend into the domain of values. In "Porcelain Cups" the order
of excellence is poetry first, chivalry, a close second, and gallantry, last.

The instrument for this evaluation is the classic pattern of the ·
comedy of manners—the witty woman and her suitors. But in
this case the witty woman, Cynthia Allonby, is shallow-minded
and spiritually void, a selfish coquette who plays destructively
with her lovers and is naïvely unconscious of her cruelty. She
has kept George Bulmer, Earl of Pevensey, from carrying out
the important mission in France with which Queen Elizabeth
has entrusted him. Jealous of Kit Marlowe's muse, she tells
Marlowe she has burned the only copy of his greatest poem.
Disgusted by the twisted perspectives of her jillflirt's will-to-
power, he plunges into dissipation at the Golden Hind. When
Captain Edward Musgrave brings Cynthia the news of Bulmer's
death from the plague and Marlowe's murder in a brawl, she
weeps decorously, then shrugs off the double tragedy, and decides that the stalwart, down-to-earth, well-to-do Musgrave will
make a good husband.

The two Chinese porcelain cups that Bulmer gives Cynthia
before his departure, along with the hand-mirror which she
places on the shelf with them, provide meaningful symbols to
unify the tale and to serve as prisms for its nuances. When Bulmer informs Cynthia that he must put duty to his country above
his attendance upon her, she complains that men of his chivalrous stamp regard women as precious cups to be kept on a shelf.
When Marlowe denounces Cynthia, he refers to the cups con-
temptuously as representative of her values. When Cynthia
reaches for her mirror to prettify herself for Musgrave and
smashes both the cups, she is grieved "by the loss of her quaint
toys," but she accepts Musgrave's gallant view that they are
only "kickshaws" and accompanies him to supper. Just as her
vanity has broken these cups, so has it collaborated with chance
to send both Bulmer and Marlowe to their deaths. Only the poet
has grasped her true essence—" 'just a bland and invincible and,
upon the whole, a well-meaning stupidity, informing a bright
and soft and delicately scented animal.' "[3]

Materialism, modishness, compromise, common sense—all receive rebuke in "Porcelain Cups," both from Marlowe's unspar-
ing candor and Cabell's urbane irony. Musgrave's clever rational-
izing that Bulmer, or Pevensey, " 'did not take proper care of

himself'" and that Marlowe merely "'wanted a pretext for making a beast of himself'" convinces the reader of the immense superiority of their intensities and integrities to his own smug "realism." The "'honest earthenware tankard'" he prefers to porcelain cups marks him as the kind of gallant who is four-fifths Philistine.[4]

II *Something About Eve*

The protagonist of *Something About Eve,* a major romance, is Gerald Musgrave. A poet in the Lichfield of 1805—when the reader first meets him—he has already fallen short of his dream through his own weakness and the trap of his place and period. He has begun a romance about Dom Manuel of Poictesme that he hopes will be a major contribution to American literature, but he has finished only one-third of it. His thoughts have turned from literature to magic. The hard work of composition is becoming less attractive than the facile hocus-pocus of working miracles with familiar spirits. But the main distraction is his adulterous involvement with Evelyn, the wife of his friend Frank Townsend.

This involvement—set forth in detail in the first of the romance's twelve movements, "The Book of Outset"—constitutes one of Cabell's most original variations on the theme of chivalry and gallantry as codes of the southern past which impede the creative artist. For in Evelyn's hold on Gerald is seen the influence of both codes in ironical collusion.

The amour began in the spirit of gallantry, but since the lovers are social equals, it must continue in the spirit of chivalry. By the peculiar ordinances of this early Virginian polite society, it is not possible to follow the sensible rule of gallantry: "'Repentance when suitably timed in a liaison makes for everybody's happiness.'"[5] Rather, one's mistress in this case must be cherished as one's lady "in domnei," according to "'the chivalrous sacrament.'"[6] Such cherishing—since Evelyn Townsend is as insatiable as Jurgen's Anaïtis—means a perpetual, enervating stallionship, in which poor Gerald is decorously encouraged by his peers—including both Evelyn's father and husband—and from which he apparently can obtain no relief or release, so long as he remains a gentleman.

The ensuing *Comedy of Fig-Leaves* concerns what happens to Gerald when this improbable relief or release actually occurs. The Guivric who traded his physical body for the demonic body of the Sylvan, Glaum of the Haunting Eyes, in *The Silver Stallion,* now appears to Gerald in his library to afford him the opportunity of another kind of stallionship. The Sylvan is ready to repeat in reverse the trade made centuries ago. He will take over Gerald's body, as well as his bedroom and library activities, while Gerald goes riding to Antan on Kalki, the silver Pegasus. Since this Antan is the ultimate country of the imagination, the realm of essence, the home of myths, gods, and poets, Gerald—through Horvendile's doing—is being offered his second chance to succeed as a creative artist.

At first it seems that he may make the most of this second chance because of his new-found chastity. Evelyn has taught him so much about sex that he knows it is only a distraction. So rather than emulating Jurgen, he deals unfairly with a number of preternatural Evelyns—Evadne of the Dusk, Evasherah of the Water-Gap, Evarvan of the Mirror, and Evaine of Peter's Tomb. In quest of a third truth beyond the limits of human living and the marches that lead to Antan, he challenges the two truths of copulation and death. He decisively affronts the supreme arbiters of existence, the organs of reproduction—the yoni and lingam symbolized by Koleos Koleros and the Holy Nose of Lytreia.

Another premise of his success is his appreciation not only of the needs of reality but also of the potentialities of romance. The land of Lytreia—or reality—is a wasteland to which he brings new life. The city of Caer Omn (romance), which is the capital of the land of Dersam (dreams), has a huge mirror with whose mythic giants he identifies completely in their age-old strife against "the malevolence of Heaven."[7] He is successively, in these "Confusions of the Golden Travel," Prometheus, Solomon, Odysseus, Judas, Nero, Tannhäuser, Villon, Faust, Don Juan, Manuel, and Jurgen. Such empathy augurs well for the quality of his imagination.

Still a third promise of his success is his refusal to be disheartened by encounters in the land of Turoine—or routine. Here are fellow magicians, literary critics, and the Sphinx of materialism itself. All represent destructive thinking of one kind or another. Gerald passes them by uncowed. His proof against their futilitarianism speaks well for the soundness of his judgment.

Then comes the supreme test in the place of compromise—Mispec Moor. Here, unlike his prototype Madoc, Gerald succumbs to Maya of the Fair Breasts, the guise which Aesred or

Aderes or Sereda assumes in order to turn into contented animals those travelers to Antan whom she can persuade to sojourn with her. Since Gerald is a special case, she is most circumspect in her dealings with him and wins him by other devices than sexual allure or aggression.

A Philistine Circe, she transforms him into a domesticated husband who sits on the porch of her cottage "half drowsily" and "so utterly comfortable in the spectacles and the dressing-gown and the brown carpet slippers which Maya had provided, and so pleasantly replete with Maya's excellent cooking."[8] She procures him a son, Theodorick Quentin Musgrave, of whom Gerald becomes inordinately fond and to whom he ultimately lends his stallion Kalki to complete the brief journey to Antan. Gerald himself never gets there.

While Gerald resides on Mispec Moor, the romance—having teetered into disguised confession in this treatment of a marriage that has some resemblance to Cabell's experience of domesticity with Priscilla Bradley—also becomes an anatomy. As action creaks to a standstill, Gerald holds odd conversations with various other travelers who stop briefly at Maya's cottage.

Nero and Villon illustrate the opposed potentialities of the human spirit as envisioned, respectively, by diabolism and by optimism. Odysseus, Solomon, and Merlin show that the masculine dreamer becomes ultimately restless with the offerings of woman—whether in the form of a wife or a harem or a mistress. Gaston Bulmer, Evelyn Townsend's father and himself a magician, pleads with Gerald to return and restore Evelyn's situation to the wonted gallant-chivalrous-Philistine respectability it is losing, he feels, with a demon for her lover.

Tannhäuser's eternal bohemian antinomianism is brought into contrast with Gerald's new-found complacent humanism. Gerald's Episcopalian God, who has ceased to believe in his own existence because of his difficulties with the Doctrine of the Trinity, is happy to be restored to his ancient simpler status as a local Arabian storm god. Finally, the Brown Man—Pan or the Prince of Darkness—functions as an antiromantic iconoclast.

In conjunction with Maya and abetted by Gerald's weakness for normal creature comforts, this Janicot has contrived Gerald's defeat, the funking of his second chance to succeed as a creative artist. In fact, the Antan that Gerald thought was his appointed kingdom—with its Master Philologist, its Queen Freydis; and its population of discarded myths, cashiered gods, and dead poets—vanishes from the horizon in a great earthquake and conflagration. His dream is ended.

With this realization, Gerald is glad to return to his natural body, which the Sylvan, Glaum, obligingly vacates. Like *Figures of Earth, Jurgen,* and *The High Place, Something About Eve* closes where it opened. In his library, Gerald finds himself an aging ethnologist who has won an international reputation with tomes produced by the industrious Glaum on the sexual customs of mankind. Glaum becomes a young poet preparing to ride to Antan on Horvendile's silver stallion. Gerald destroys the unfinished romance about Dom Manuel, which the Sylvan has left untouched, and gets in the mood to resume his relations with his Egeria, Evelyn, whom the years have made less exigent in nymphomania.

To the departing Glaum—as earlier to Horvendile—Gerald defends his failure. The unattained always keeps its glamor. Living with Maya had its compensations. But the reader's final view of Gerald, through the preternatural eyes of Glaum, with their "half-lazy, mildly humorous mockery,"[9] is one of pity. He will never be a great poet or even a formidable magician. He will cackle contentedly graveward as a fairly well-known, pedantic scholar who in his off moments plays at being a poetaster.

Something About Eve, Cabell has stated, "is the story . . . I wrote with the largest portion of ease and zest."[10] Evidence that he had let himself go abounds. Such chapters as "The Holy Nose of Lytreia" and "Confusions of the Golden Travel" have already been cited as showing his salacity and his rhetoric, respectively, in their most rampageous fettle. Gerald's magnificent diatribe against law in the chapter entitled "At Tenjo's Table" runs these a close second. The dialogue of Evaine of Peter's Tomb is also worthy of mention. This incredible Fox-Spirit explains all her allusions as if she had been working on a dictionary or an anthology and had a compulsion to compose definitions and annotations. Seldom has the learned lady or the female pseudo-intellectual been hit off with greater gusto. The chapter called "A Boy that Might Be" contains a delightful exchange between Gerald and his son. Theodorick Quentin calls his father's attention to the fact that the landscape "expansed" from Mispec Moor in the direction of Antan looks like a recumbent nude whose heart is breathing. Gerald doesn't catch on at first; but, when he observes closely, notes all the contours, and discerns a forest fire languidly smoking near the hill slope forming the left breast, he is elate with paternal pride. These are but a few of the many choice bits in a book well stocked with waggeries and preciosities.

III *The Certain Hour*

The Certain Hour, a collection of ten tales with an extended "Auctorial Induction" and ballads that appear also in *From the Hidden Way* serving as prologue and epilogue, has the same function with reference to the poetic attitude that *Chivalry* and *Gallantry* have with reference to *their* attitudes. Less restricted in time, it ranges all the way from the thirteenth to the late nineteenth centuries. The ten poets treated—some historical personages and others fictitious—are identified with the clay figures that Dom Manuel shaped and that Queen Freydis endowed with life, sending them to move among mankind as changelings.

Their changeling role accounts for one of Cabell's main theses in the collection. He is attempting to demonstrate that poets who succeed in the way of poetry—those who create enduring works—tend to fail as human beings. Each of these ten, he asserts, is in this respect a contrast to Gerald Musgrave of *Something About Eve,* who put his Pegasus out to graze while spending many years of pleasant, normal married life with his Maya of the Fair Breasts on Mispec Moor. Whereas Gerald didn't reach Antan, no one of these ten can forget that he came from there.

Another main thesis of the collection is that poets, being more sensitive than normal human beings, are more affected by their surroundings. Their works and their personalities thus reflect and epitomize their times as the activities and identities of average folk do not. Each of the ten, by the very fact of his creativity, is a clue to his era and also a puppet of his period.

At first glance, the two theses seem entirely incompatible. One of them calls attention to the alienation of the genuine literary artist from the world; this thesis is derived from nineteenth-century romanticism in its more decadent, negative, aesthetic phase. The other thesis stresses the conditioning of the literary artist and his art by the *Zeitgeist,* a thesis traceable to nineteenth-century naturalistic thinking with its commitment to sociological and psychological determinism. On second thought, the incompatibility of the theses becomes an affinity conducive to unifying, challenging irony. The plight of the true poet is revealed in all its tragi-comic complexity—a complexity that Poe's "Israfel," with its commingling of Platonic aspiration and environmental fatality, merely suggests but does not develop.

Cabell's actual development of it in these tales is somewhat uneven. The tale, by its very nature, limits him to a certain hour in each poet's career. So limited, he cannot usually treat the poet's work, personality, and age with the equal justice that the ironical dichotomy of these theses demands. So he concentrates on the personality as the certain hour highlights it, rings in the age by implication, and trusts that, in the case of historical poets, the reader can supply knowledge of the work, or, in the case of fictitious poets, take it for granted. The only thing certain about most of the hours, generally speaking, is that each involves a woman; and such involvement has the demerit not only of monotony but also of disintegrating the poetic attitude into vague, confusing variations of chivalry or gallantry.

The last point applies particularly not only to "Belhs Cavaliers," in which the thirteenth-century troubadour Raimbaut de Vaqueiras is overnice about honor, but also to "Balthazar's Daughter," in which the early sixteenth-century Duke Alessandro de Medici—as has already been seen in *The Jewel Merchants*—is overdevilish in his lust. In "Olivia's Pottage," Wycherley is truer, in an amorous imbroglio of his later years, to the spirit of seventeenth-century gallantry than he had been in his most gallant comedies. In "Pro Honoria," the eighteenth-century Ufford displays, as an intriguer violating the Seventh Commandment, the kind of boomeranging extremism he had lambasted in his satires. In "The Irresistible Ogle," Sheridan, with a philanthropic female burglar as partner, carries out in life high jinks of eighteenth-century gallantry which are more uproariously amusing than anything in his three dramatic masterpieces.

In "Judith's Creed" and "The Lady of All Our Dreams," two writers who have modified their art to give the public what it wants confront the women who inspired their earlier, more uncompromising creativity. They react differently, according to the relative strength and weakness of their changeling natures.

Shakespeare, in his garden at Stratford, is working on *The Tempest*, which is inspired in part by the demands of his seventeenth-century audience for happy endings and in part by what he takes to be the creed of his daughter Judith, who is living in the "brave new world" of first love. The Dark Lady of the *Sonnets*—identified with the same Cynthia Allonby whom we have seen playing with Kit Marlowe in "Porcelain Cups"—comes to remind Shakespeare of their passionate past. But he rejects that past as an important experience to him as a human being. It has served its purpose to shape the poems and some of the tragedies he once wrote. "'Lord, what a deal of ruined life it takes to make a little art!'" is his summary.[11] Now he has turned to other, more optimistic productions in the composition of which he still finds a craftsman's joy, even though they no longer express the essential Shakespeare at his zenith—the Shakespeare to whom the Dark Lady was as Cressida to Troilus or Cleopatra to Antony.

John Charteris, now a successful novelist whose preciously phrased prevarications about life are very much to the taste of a late nineteenth-century American reading public, goes to sleep on the campus of King's College in Fairhaven after having delivered a Commencement Address. In a dream his quondam college love Pauline Romeyne returns, like Shakespeare's Dark Lady, to remind him of their lost high-hearted yesterday. Taking this dream for reality and this fanciful Pauline—who says she is still unmarried—for the actual Pauline of the present, Charteris would persuade her to help him "'tweak the nose of Time intrepidly'" and "'know the Dream again,'" when she suddenly departs and he is awakened by his friend Rudolph Musgrave. Musgrave tells him that the actual Pauline is now the wife of old General Ashmeade and "'was the very fat gray-haired woman in purple who carried out her squalling brat'" when Charteris was being introduced to his Commencement audience.[12]

"Concerning Corinna" tells how Herrick, brought back from the preternatural world to which his changeling spirit has effected a return through seventeenth-century occult practices, prefers suicide to continued human life. "A Princess in Grub Street" records the rebellion of the early nineteenth-century poet Paul Vanderhoffen and his sweetheart Mildred Claridge against the stultification that high social position and its responsibilities impose on the creative impulse. He gives up a grand dukedom to be free to write verses; she is willing to forego a fashionable marriage to become his princess in Grub Street. The implication at the close of the story, however, is that to support his princess he will have to put his muse in the service of literary hackwork. Eluding one pitfall for the poet in an age of power politics and revolution, he has fallen into another dug by sentiment. Can his changeling spirit survive it?

Perhaps the most successful tale in the collection is "A Brown Woman," which opposes to the disappointments, fortuitous catastrophes, and essential transience of human living, the perdurability of poetic achievement. Pope, falling in love with the charming country girl Sarah Drew, discovers that she loves her rustic swain, John Hughes (Cabell's name for the actual John Hewet). So Pope generously makes it possible for them to marry. When the news comes that they have been struck dead by lightning, the circumstance inspires him to a mixed meditation. " 'I shall not perish thus entirely, I believe. Men will remember me,' " he observes. But then he castigates his poet's pride: " '. . . the utmost I can hope for is but to be read in one island, and to be thrown aside at the end of one age. Indeed, I am not even sure of that much. I print, and print, and print. And when I collect my verses into books, I am altogether uncertain . . . to look upon myself as a man building a monument, or burying the dead.' " In the end, however, he and John Gay set about writing a *pastorelle* concerning Sarah and her swain "which has to-day its proper rating among Mr. Pope's Complete Works."[13] The composition to which Cabell refers is the epitaph, "On Two Lovers Struck Dead by Lightning." It survives in three versions, and Gay may have had a hand in two of them.

IV *The Eagle's Shadow and The Cream of the Jest*

The same Richard Fentnor Harrowby who has been mentioned as the compiler of *The Rivet in Grandfather's Neck* is the omniscient chronicler of the two comedies, *The Eagle's Shadow* and *The Cream of the Jest*. Harrowby, as one of the many young men vulnerable to the charm of Margaret Hugonin, heroine of *The Eagle's Shadow*, tells something about himself before its opening curtain, but he warns the reader that he has "no part whatever in her story." Writing from the perspective of age, he invests this story with the aura of nostalgic reminiscence. It belongs to "the ineffably remote, strange days of Colonel Roosevelt's first presidential term"—"that departed and callow and dear time. . . ."[14] If one wants to know more about Harrowby, one has to turn to the last volume of the "Biography," where he is the first-person protagonist of the tale, "Concerning David Jogram: A Survival in Saccharine." Here his sweetheart Moira Knapman conjures him by degrees from complacent attachment into vexed ardor by inventing a rival—the Jogram of the title.

The main action of *The Eagle's Shadow,* Cabell's first published book and first long fiction, is also—even in its considerably revised form in the "Biography"—a "survival in saccharine" and has only a superficial relation to his later concern with chivalry or gallantry as definite attitudes. Margaret Hugonin, daughter of a humorously old-fogyish English colonel, has inherited the large fortune and spacious country estate, "Selwoode," near Fairhaven—or Williamsburg, Virginia—of the Wall Street tycoon, Frederick R. Woods, her uncle by marriage. His blood nephew, William Vartrey Woods, should have been the heir, but Billy's refusal to obey his uncle's command to marry Margaret led to his being disinherited. Having come of age, Margaret patronizes "philanthropy and literature and theosophy and art and temperance and education and all other laudable causes"[15] and distrusts the motives of her several suitors. Billy, who went to Paris as a painter, returns on the day the curtain rises. Despite his earlier rejection of Margaret and her subsequent disdain of him, they are actually very much in love with each other.

Their love story, played at the "Selwoode" house-party that insures all the unities, is an ingeniously contrived duel of the sexes replete with amusing complications and reversals. Three wills, several marriage proposals (one unintentional), eavesdropping in a summer-house, and a staff-wielding, larcenous thug named Cock-eye Flints sent by a mysterious Orven Deal (Horvendile)—all these provide the suspense and eventually produce the expected happy ending. As the subtitle—*A Comedy of Purse-Strings*—suggests, the prevailing mood is quasi-gallant rather than chivalrous. Although there are echoes of Shakespeare, Congreve, and Meredith, neither Margaret nor Billy—however delightful each may be as a young person of the period—is especially witty. Such remarks as the following reveal the calibre of Margaret's intellect at its most unconventional: " 'I hate poetry, anyhow,—it is so mushy.' "—" 'Women's clubs are silly, and I think the women who belong to them are bold-faced jigs! . . . I don't want to be cultured,—I want to be happy.' " Billy's most sprightly utterance occurs when he is delirious from being knocked unconscious by Cock-eye Flints: " 'Uncle Fred should not have left so many wills,—who would have thought the old man had so much ink in him?' "[16]

The minor action or subplot, however, does have an important bearing on Cabell's development of the way of poetry. For its central character is Felix Bulmer Kennaston, in his late thirties, the author of three "emaciated volumes of verse"[17] and of a forthcoming book of Wildean prose, *Defence of Ignorance*. Margaret has subsidized his publications and values him as a friend. His conception of the poetic attitude reflects the aestheticism of the 1890's.

The chapter entitled "The Menagerie is Fed" brings his aestheticism into contrast with the utilitarianism of Margaret's other guests as well as with that of Margaret herself. Mrs. Kathleen Eppes Saumarez, the widow of a Spaniard, lectures before women's clubs and writes "sympathetic stories of Nature and animal life." Petheridge Jukesbury is "president of the Society for the Suppression of Nicotine and the Nude, vice-president of the Anti-Inebriation League, and secretary of the Society for the Eradication of the Erotic." Mrs. Sarah Ellen Haggage is "President General of the Society for Sexless Suffrage, the third Vice-Regent of the Daughters of All American Wars, and a Director of the Ladies League for the Edification of the Impecunious." Margaret, as their patron, is—according to Kennaston—" 'casting whole bakeryfuls of bread upon the waters of philanthropy.' " He refers to himself as " 'horribly out of place . . . the idle singer of an empty day,—a mere drone in this hive of philanthropic bees.' "[18]

The chapter called "Which Flouts Veracity" puts his aestheticism in opposition to the scientific spirit of the day and its fetish of truth-telling. Kennaston reads to the assembled company from his *Defence of Ignorance*. Its burden is that " 'The true poet must be ignorant, since information is the grief of rhyme.' "[19] Too much concern for facts has robbed mythology of its imaginative potency, nature of its mystery, and history of its heroism. Pedantry is everywhere supplanting creativity.

Finally, in the chapter "Mr. Kennaston Speaks the Parabasis," he flays, with the cat-o'-nine-tails of his aestheticism, the capitalistic, industrial materialism of the age. His point of departure is the eagle which a professional genealogist employed by tycoon Frederick discovered to be the heraldic blazoning on the Woods's coat-of-arms. This eagle is inescapable at "Selwoode," since it is "carved in the woodwork . . . set in the mosaics . . . chased in the tableware . . . woven in the napery . . . glazed in the china." But Kennaston has another eagle in mind. Producing a dollar bill, he shows Margaret that it bears "'the original of the Woods Eagle.'" In other words, the shadow that broods over "Selwoode" and over factories in the South, sweatshops, mines, Wall Street, and the whole modern world is the curse of exploitative wealth. He makes the following wry prophecy: "'But there must be an end some day, with a quite glorious smash-up, all around, and such heroic havoc as will find me, I hope, already snugly tucked into a comfortable coffin. My faith in this revolution's inevitability, you see, is qualified by my sense of being just the sort of person that revolutionists kill first of all.'"[20]

His interest in a coffin, however, is largely metaphorical. He still has enough zest for life to propose to Kathleen Saumarez, explaining to her, "'For fifteen years now I have rubbed along without ever being able to fall in love with you or do without you——'" Her opinion of him has not been flattering: "'Your life is nothing but a succession of poses,—of shallow, foolish poses meant to hoodwink the world and at times yourself.'" But still she loves him. So she accepts him after he has assured her that he has no entangling alliances with Muriel Allardyce, Marian Winwood, and a couple of others she knows about.[21]

After Harrowby's brief introduction, *The Cream of the Jest* opens in Poictesme with Horvendile playing a diabolic and decisive role in the rivalry of Sir Guiron des Rocques and Maugis d'Aigremont for the possession of Ettarre. Then, with only slight foreshadowing, the reader finds him walking slowly, not through the gardens of Storisende, but through those of Alcluid, which is the odd name of the fine country home near Lichfield inherited by Felix Kennaston along with a sufficient fortune to make him independent. The Horvendile whose tribute to Ettarre in contrapuntal prose has turned the reader's silent reading into cadenced mumbling is an imagined avatar of Kennaston. As the author among his puppets, Kennaston has been living the life of Satan's red-headed clerk. Now he has returned to assume the personality of a successful author who owns two automobiles, keeps his money in four banks, is comfortably married to his Kathleen, and has gone beyond the ninetyish verse and essay-writing attributed to him in *The Eagle's Shadow* to produce such a distinguished prose romance as *The Audit at Storisende,* finally to be published as *Men Who Loved Alison.*

Flight into dream, return to actuality—this dualistic pattern of the poet's living recurs continually as one goes on reading. The dream-world that Kennaston revisits over and over again, both in sleep and in the reveries of his waking hours, extends beyond medieval Poictesme into many eras of a remoter or a more recent past. These moments into which he enters compel his and the reader's willing suspension of disbelief, even when they are merely fragmentary, with antecedents and outcomes that remain obscure. Ettarre, the eternal witch-woman, the deathless symbol of that elusive supernal Beauty which the human imagination forever yearns after without being able to possess utterly, is ubiquitous in this dreaming, wearing one or another of her innumerable legendary, historical, or literary guises. In comparison with any one of these moments in the realm of essence, the experiences of actuality—with publishers and critics, or with domesticity or "society," or in re-encountering such a woman of his past as Muriel Allardyce, or in conferring with an eminent contemporary statesman or ecclesiastic, or in arguing with his friend Harrowby—are relatively humdrum. But some of the mystery of that other world occasionally intrudes in the most unexpected, curious, and puzzling ways.

By his legacy emancipated from truckling to the gallery gods, Kennaston has some resemblance to the mature Ernest Pontifex of the closing pages of Butler's *The Way of All Flesh.* Harrowby, functioning as an intruding narrator, supports this resemblance by vaguely recalling to the reader the wiser, more aphoristic Mr. Overton of Butler's novel. Obsessed with Poictesme—"that fair country, very far from Lichfield, which is bounded by Avalon and Phaeacia and Sea-coast Bohemia, and the contiguous forests of Arden and Broceliande, and on the west, of course, by the Hesperides"[22]—Kennaston is like Lucian Taylor, in Arthur Machen's *The Hill of Dreams,* rapt in the ecstasy of Roman Caermaen. Exploring a library well stocked with recondite volumes and evolving his exotic theories of cosmology, human evolution, and aesthetics, Kennaston has some of the eccentricity although little of the decadence of J. K. Huysmans' Des Esseintes in *Against the Grain*—the "poisonous" "yellow book" that Lord Henry sent to his Charmides in Wilde's *The Picture of Dorian Gray.*[23] Entering into so many bygone lives as virtually to epito-

mize humanity and its irrational history, Kennaston faintly echoes
the protagonists of two romances of reincarnation—Edwin Lester
Arnold's *Phra the Phoenician* and Jack London's *The Star Rover*.
Because of his escapism and the ironic surprises of actuality that
eventually overtake it, Kennaston's story is appropriately subtitled
A Comedy of Evasion. Since he is comfortably married—unlike
any of the other characters to whom he has been compared—
his story might also have been called "A Portrait of the Artist
as An Aging Schizoid Husband."

Thackeray in "De Finibus," one of the most self-revealing of
his *Roundabout Papers*, tells how the characters of his creation
became real people to him, moved into his study, disrupted his
household, ignored his convenience, and behaved generally with
wills of their own. If one combines this view of the author's
relation to his puppets with Coleridge's primary and secondary
imagination and if one adds the Butlerian, Shavian, and Berg-
sonian versions of "creative evolution," he has the substance of
Kennaston's thinking about art and reality.

Human beings in history are to God what the characters in
a fiction in progress are to the writer. The fiction grows shapelier,
more convincing, more exciting slowly—with many false starts,
bungled chapters, and discarded pages—as the writer moves his
characters and as they move in on him. Life is God's form of
self-expression, determined by his intentions but also imposing
itself on these intentions and changing them, sometimes for the
worse, but ultimately for the better, in an endless struggle toward
perfection through experiment, revision, metamorphosis, and
transubstantiation. The process is uncertain, anguished, even
maddening; but it is fraught with both minor and major miracles.
One must preserve faith in its eventual outcome. In the two chapters of *The Cream of the Jest* entitled " 'Epper Si Muove,' " and
"Evolution of a Vestryman," Cabell has translated the theology
of Jonathan Edwards' *A Dissertation Concerning the End for
Which God Created the World* into the terms of twentieth-century aesthetic historicism.

The contrast with *The Eagle's Shadow* is marked. Whereas
the latter is social comedy at its lightest, the comedy of *The
Cream of the Jest* moves toward the cosmic. The action of *The
Eagle's Shadow* is too neatly plotted, but *The Cream of the Jest*
has only fragments of action and no plot line. To achieve what
Conrad and Ford Madox Ford called *"progression d'effet"* and

what E. M. Forster has termed "rhythm," Cabell resorts to two symbols and one phrase that are repeated with variations. The symbols are the mysterious sigil of Scoteia, broken into two halves, and the even more puzzling mumbo-jumbo involving a mirror and pigeons. The phrase is the title itself, which is worked into the text at regular intervals with different implications.[24] Cabell uses such devices with all the finesse of Conrad in *Chance,* Ford in *The Good Soldier,* and Forster in *Howards End.*[25]

Contrast with *Something About Eve* is also worth pointing out. Gerald Musgrave failed as a poet but attended to his responsibilities as a human being with considerable enjoyment and success; Kennaston was much more of a success as a poet in both verse and prose. Though he wrote only a few books, their quality was high. But as a human being he was considerably less successful, going through the motions of a happy marriage rather than entering into its deeper satisfactions. On the other hand, the reader's conception of the true value of marriage is vastly different as he explores the two works. In *Something About Eve,* marriage is a compromise inimical to the development of the creative power of the poet or artist. *The Cream of the Jest* carries Kennaston to the discovery that Kathleen has the other, missing half of the sigil of Scoteia and that, when the halves are put together, they are nothing but the top of a jar in which is sold a brand of cold cream widely used by women. Kathleen drops the broken top into a wastebasket by her dressing-table. Later, however, she recovers the halves and preserves them, as Kennaston finds after she has died suddenly in her sleep. They meant to her what the sigil had meant to him. The magic, exotic piece of metal, by which he induced his dreams, was a commonplace household article. Supreme happiness was at home instead of in Poictesme. Kathleen was Ettarre —if he had only had the insight to perceive it. The curdled "cream of the jest" is that he became aware of this simple truth too late.

Thus, the way of poetry, as the reader finally understands it in this last fiction in the design of the "Biography," is not the way of changelinghood, of demonic estrangement and escape, but the way of sanely human acceptance after soaring retreat and safe return. Although Cabell may sometimes seem the Miniver Cheevy of modern American literature, his wisdom is not too far from Frost's in "Birches."

CHAPTER 6

Later Writings

AFTER an author has spent the better part of his creative life
bringing to completion an ambitious series of works, anything
that he writes later is usually an addendum or postscript. Its
main interest lies in the extension or modification of themes or
motifs or the further development of forms with which he has
already become identified. These generalizations apply, for example, to the trilogy of "The Three Cities" and to the unfinished
tetralogy of "The Four Gospels" to which Zola devoted his ener-
gies after making fictional history with the twenty novels of the
Rougon-Macquart series. And Cabell's numerous writings after
the "Biography" are another case in point.

One purpose of the present chapter is to review them so as
to clarify this point in some detail. A caution, however, is necessary. Too often, the inevitably repetitive character of a copious
author's final efforts dooms them as dotages, and critics fail,
therefore, to assess them in isolation or for themselves. Invidious
comparison operates automatically before a fair hearing. A second purpose of this chapter is to rescue Cabell's later writings
from such premature aspersion or dismissal. This study respec-
fully keeps in mind what Cabell in his last fiction, *The Devil's
Own Dear Son*, says of his Jehovah's anger at adverse judgment
of his post-seraphic fashionings: ". . . no creative artist can
bear to be told that his current compositions are inferior to his
early work."[1]

I *The Essayist*

As has been pointed out earlier, both *Beyond Life* and *Straws
and Prayer-Books* contain discussions of writers that indicate
Cabell's keen interest in literary criticism. The incorporation of
these discussions into the prologue and epilogue of the "Biography" shows that Cabell was an economist in a somewhat more
literal sense than that meant in his theory of the poet. Cabell's

economy consisted in never, if he could help it, letting any scrap of his writings, however fugitive, go unused in book form. A college essay on Congreve; book reviews such as that of Donn Byrne's *Messer Marco Polo* or of the Carra Edition of George Moore; the introduction done for the Modern Library edition of Anatole France's *The Queen Pédaque*—all these had to be salvaged and worked into the larger argument expounding the "Biography's" intentions or justifying its existence.

As a literary critic, Cabell is an impressionist, striving to recreate, as vividly as possible, his personal sense of his subject's world as it mirrors its creator's personality. His models are the Pater of *Appreciations* and the Wilde of the "purple patch" digressions in "The Critic as Artist" in *Intentions*. This type of criticism—so different from the close analysis that the so-called "new critics" have caused to prevail—has its place, as David Daiches has demonstrated in his *Critical Approaches to Literature*. It can inspire readers to recall or to revisit works they have enjoyed, or it can enhance their ability to enter into the spirit of works or fictive worlds they have not yet explored. Such criticism is at its best when dealing with writers congenial to the critic—writers whose selves reflect facets of his own.

After the "Biography," Cabell's chief venture in such criticism was *Some of Us: An Essay in Epitaphs*. His purpose in this volume—anticipated to some extent in the "Biography" 's appendix piece, *Townsend of Lichfield*—is to defend himself and several of his fellow writers of the 1920's against the attacks of neo-humanists and other apostles of some form of ethical or social conformity for the writer. The basis of his defense is aesthetic individualism. The essays most successful in implementing this defense through vivid appreciation of their subjects' individual quality are those on Elinor Wylie, Frances Newman, Ellen Glasgow, Sinclair Lewis, Joseph Hergesheimer, and H. L. Mencken. Such strokes as the apostrophe to Lewis' Babbitt in terms of a parody of Pater on the Mona Lisa, or the labeling of Mencken's clamorous disciples as the "Menckenoids," or the scrupulous unlinking and later strategic coupling of Mr. George F. Babbitt of Zenith and Mr. Irving Babbitt of Cambridge are not soon forgotten.[2]

An unpardonable lapse in the conduct of the defense is the one-page chapter, "Remarks in Transit," which begins with the gambit, "I perceive some merit in Willa Cather,"[3] and then proceeds to explain that his unfamiliarity with her work makes it impossible for him to discuss it. Cabell thus convicts himself of either indolence or snobbery or both, and he also calls into question his competence to speak for the decade he claims to represent. Never was a jousting champion more truant to chivalry, more renegade to a lady in whose behalf he had pledged himself to wield a lance.

Cabell's prefaces to each volume of the "Biography" blending interpretation of his own work with fragments of autobiography were later collected—with minor revisions and supplements—in *Preface to the Past,* making a volume precursory to Ellen Glasgow's *A Certain Measure. Straws and Prayer-Books,* as already mentioned, combined tales and auctorial meditations. The epistles to Mrs. Grundy introducing *The Line of Love* and *Gallantry* showed Cabell's mastery of this semi-formal expository device for elaborating his ideas with overtones of irony. All these minor features of the "Biography" prepared for his later major achievement in the essay—the trilogy called "Their Lives and Letters" and consisting of *These Restless Heads: A Trilogy of Romantics, Special Delivery: A Packet of Replies,* and *Ladies and Gentlemen: A Parcel of Reconsiderations.*

The most beautifully structured of these volumes is *These Restless Heads.* A tale treating the aging Prospero's decision to return to his island and take up once more his put-by magic-making serves as prologue. Then Cabell—another Prospero—favors the reader with his reflections during all four seasons of a typical year in his creative life. The third "restless head" is that of Thomas Learmont, also a romantic well past his prime: the epilogue is a tale of his last dealings with the Queen of Faëry.

The aesthetic individualism defended in *Some of Us* is everywhere in evidence in *These Restless Heads.* Its best expressions are in contrasts of flags and women. Turning his back on the Stars and Stripes, Cabell dreams—not of the Stars and Bars—but of a national banner to which he can be truly loyal, that of Poictesme with its ramping silver stallion. The pallid bust that presides over his writing desk at home is that of Aesred, whose role both in the mythology of Poictesme and in the history of literature, especially English, he memorably reviews. But his reading glasses play tricks with the all-powerful goddess of compromise and conformity, transforming her into Ettarre. And it is as a postulant of Ettarre rather than as a servant of Aesred that he eagerly begins a new paragraph.

Special Delivery presents the letters Cabell would have liked to send in answer to correspondents, if he had had the time, along with the conventional replies he actually did send. This amusing basic schema permits him to bring together an extraordinarily diverse series of observations, some concerning art and life in general and others bearing on particular points in his own life and books. Some are *tours de force* of satire and irony. "Grace Abundant," for example, does a thorough job of saying "Scat!"[4] to one of those ardent, immature young women who yearn for an affair with him. "About Loveliness Revised" subjects to withering candor the sentimental nostalgia of an ex-mistress of long ago.

Ladies and Gentlemen, a series of epitaph-like epistles to dead persons, is probably indebted to Andrew Lang's *Letters to Dead Authors.* But Cabell ranges far more widely, reduces authors to a minimum, is most interested in historical figures who have given rise to legends and myths, and even includes beings mainly fictitious. Lang writes to Thackeray, Dickens, Ronsard, Herodotus, Pope, Lucian, Rabelais, Jane Austen, Isaak Walton, Chapelain, Sir John Mandeville, Dumas *père,* Theocritus, Poe, Sir Walter Scott, Eusebius, Shelley, Molière, Burns, Byron, Omar Khayyám, and Horace; but Cabell addresses the following familiar spirits: Penelope, Tutankhamen, Solomon, Egeria, Jonah, Julius Caesar, Ananias, Sir Galahad, Geoffrey Rudel, Timur the Splendid, Falstaff, Dr. Faustus, Pocahontas, Richard Cabell, George Washington, Poe, John Wilkes Booth, Madame de Pompadour, Hamlet, and Jurgen.

While each letter has points worth making and does so with consummate elegance and ease, three letters are outstanding for different reasons. One of the most original and erudite is that "To Egeria, the Fond Huntress." Her fascinating and neglected myth becomes very much alive in Cabell's hands. Two important modern novels make brilliant use of the Egeria myth or figure—James's *The Sacred Fount* and Conrad's *Under Western Eyes.* Although Cabell mentions neither, he provides excellent background for understanding both.

"To Mr. John Wilkes Booth" is one of Cabell's most provocative commentaries on American history. He gives Booth credit for doing more than anyone else to create the Lincoln myth by assassinating him at the historically and psychologically right moment. "To Edgar Allan Poe, Esq." is the most irritating of all Cabell's discussions of American literature. He cites Poe's dictum that "as a literary people, we are one vast perambulating humbug"[5] as true for Poe's time; and he then tries to show that it has remained more or less true ever since. From his blanket indictment he excepts only "A sufficing amount of Poe; and a tiny fraction of Mark Twain."[6] Before he has done, he has even included amongst the "humbug" much of Poe's Gothicism and Dickensian rhetoric.

Cabell's last trilogy containing essays—"Virginians are Various"—consists of *Let Me Lie: Being in the Main an Ethnological Account of the Remarkable Commonwealth of Virginia and the Making of Its History; Quiet, Please;* and *As I Remember It: Some Epilogues in Recollection.* Autobiographical reminiscence predominates in these volumes over straight essays. Several of the latter are critical commentaries on his own work. Since much of the reminiscence material has already been used in the first chapter of this book, further discussion is needless. Suffice it to say that *Let Me Lie,* in delving into Virginia's past, presents two of Cabell's finest letters to the illustrious dead—one to Thackeray's Colonel Esmond and the other to General Robert E. Lee; that *Quiet, Please* is skillfully unified by the theme of Time as villain; and that *As I Remember It* is an exercise in candor interesting to set alongside Ellen Glasgow's *The Woman Within* as additional evidence of the variousness of Virginians.

II   *"The Nightmare Has Triplets"*

"The Nightmare Has Triplets," a fictional trilogy, consists of *Smirt: An Urbane Nightmare; Smith: A Sylvan Interlude;* and *Smire: An Acceptance in the Third Person.* It is Cabell's *Finnegans Wake,* and it was published while Joyce's opus was still known only in fragments as *Work in Progress.* Never except in an Italian translation, *L'Incubo (The Nightmare),* with Surrealist illustrations by Fabrizio Clerici and an extended preface by Fernanda Pivano, has Cabell's trilogy been made available in one volume. Edmund Wilson has suggested that its re-issue in the United States in an "omnibus" form would be advisable to permit and encourage its being read as the unified whole that he apparently thinks it is. According to him, "We have hardly had

a chance to enjoy or to judge this amusing and original book—
of dream comedies the most opalescent."[7]

"The Nightmare"—as Cabell explains in the "Author's Note" to
Smirt and in a longer commentary in *Quiet, Please*—grew out of
two of his dissatisfactions with the "Biography": (1) its scrupulous avoidance of the method of naturalistic fiction; (2) its use
of the dream merely as a narrative device, as in *The Cream of the
Jest, The High Place, Jurgen,* and *Figures of Earth.* What
Cabell now proposed to do was to surpass Lewis Carroll by
applying the documentary veracity of Zola and his disciples to
the representative nocturnal adventures of a mature dreamer
and thus to deal justly with the entire one-third of human experience that the modern novel has chosen to ignore.

This ambitious intention accounts for the quasi-autobiographi-
cal aspect of "The Nightmare" and for some of its technical oddities. For the sake of veracity, the dreamer is a projection of
the author himself—a famous Virginian romance-writer going out
of fashion and much derided by the critics, but still annoyed
by the unintelligent flattery and irrelevant curiosity of the public
at large. His egoism, sexuality, and rhetorical fluency are relatively uninhibited. His identity, like that of a god, is constantly
dissolving. Achieving the all-powerful status of an ersatz Jehovah
in *Smirt,* he changes into a minor forest deity in *Smith* and has
his attributes reflected in four sons. He ends as the decadent
Holy Ghost in *Smire.* Time is so scrambled and telescoped that
anything not anachronistic seems improbable, and causality becomes wholly casual. Places tend to behave as did the mountain
to Mohammed. Although hearing and touch are not noticeably
impaired, sight is at once sharper and hazier than in waking
hours, while taste and smell are virtually nullified. Mythology,
history, literature, statistics, and journalism coalescently contribute to the continuing kaleidoscope of irreality.

The analogy with *Finnegans Wake* breaks down under close
scrutiny. Joyce is writing in a difficult, experimental, nonsense
language appropriate to his theme; Cabell's is a nonsense world,
but his language offers few difficulties. His prose has an ease,
flow, bounce, and clarity that make for rapid reading and quick
communication of even his dizziest fancies. Where Joyce has
wrought a labored, organically unified modern Edda founded
on Jung and Vico, Cabell has contrived a breezy, episodic, duffel-
baggish, mock-Freudian travesty well suited to his economist

practice of salvaging pieces from his workshop—in this instance, primarily tales and short anatomies.

The tales, a tetralogy, are confined to *Smith*, and they concern the sons—Volmar, Elair, Clitandre, and Little Smirt—begotten by Smirt in the first volume of the trilogy. Volmar is a chivalrous protagonist in reverse, showing his domnei to his Sonia by persistent malice. The other three are variations of the poetic protagonist. Elair—like Gerald Musgrave—enjoys domesticity with his Maya-like Oina; and he is happy to relinquish the original object of his quest, Queen Fergail—now magically re-endowed with her Ettarre-like youthful comeliness—to his son Cowan. The Villon-like Clitandre finds that his idealized court-lady Marianne and his murdered trollope Nicole are sisters under the skin. Little Smirt, the precocious scholar, is guided chastely to his Bel-Imperia by the dead hand of his mother Tana—a hand she chopped off and gave to him. Later, when his mother is in trouble as a witch, he is pathetically loyal to her; and he is rewarded for his loyalty by having restored to him both his lost father—Smith-Smirt—and his Tana in her unmutilated youth. Cabell justifies inclusion of these tales on the ground that their protagonists embody four of their god-like father's attributes— "stubborn wilfulness . . . blind self-complacency . . . inveterate poeticizing . . . pig-headed pedantry."[8] But that the tales are mainly "leftovers" from the "Biography"—and none too impressive ones at that—is all too obvious.

Some of the short anatomies are better. In *Smirt* the chapters "Lying Awake" and "Reflections of the Master" and in *Smire* the chapter "The Dark Ferryman" contain parodies of stream-of-consciousness writing. In *Smirt* the chapter entitled "Heir Presumptive" permits a young proletarian novelist to expose his arrogance, ignorance, and vulgarity and to condemn Smirt-Cabell in words borrowed from Granville Hicks in *The Great Tradition*.[9] The chapter "A Lecture for Dorothy" unleashes a diatribe against public lecturing as a suitable practice for authors. In *Smire*, the chapter "Colloquy of Animals" presents the Sheep, the Cow, and the Hog as speakers, respectively, for the human conscience, mind, and body. A succeeding chapter, "'Laugh and Lie Down,'" defines one of the central conflicts in mankind's history as that between "the great virtue of justice" and "the great virtue of charity" as symbolized in the eternal opposition of the Puritan and the Cavalier.[10] A third chapter, "Regarding the Stars," sets over against the unappreciated splendor of the heavens at night the eclipsing, garish, commercial illumination of modern cities.

Throughout "The Nightmare," Cabell aligns himself with a kind of humanism by presenting Smirt-Smith-Smire as "the Peripatetic Episcopalian" pursuing a middle way "between piety and atheism."[11] This position gives him such a talking point that all the forces of Hell are enlisted to prevent his damnation and to foist him off on Heaven. At the same time Cabell is bemused by what he takes to be a central problem of humanism—the difficulty of keeping mediation distinct from compromise. The first is discriminating and self-reliant; the second, concessive and conformist. Love at its most satisfying is a compromise to which the Peripatetic Episcopalian in all his personae eventually succumbs. Smirt forsakes his supreme position in Amit for Arachne. Smith lets Tana lull him to uninquisitive contentment in the marvelous forest of Branlon. Smire, after finding Branlon's long-lost haven enduring and intact, goes home to Jane.

III *"Heirs and Assigns"*

"Heirs and Assigns," a fictional trilogy, consists of *Hamlet Had an Uncle: A Comedy of Honor, The King Was in His Counting House: A Comedy of Common-Sense,* and *The First Gentleman of America: A Comedy of Conquest.* It relies less on invention and more on specific historical and literary sources than does most of Cabell's previous work, for many of the characters and actions and the main settings come from these sources. The form of each narrative is in some measure imitative of whatever form originally became associated with the materials as most appropriate to their rendering.

The consequence of such double indebtedness is an almost un-Cabellesque objectivity. The worlds he is inviting the reader to enter are still fantastic, but much of their fantasy is that of history or legend and not his. Structure, narrative perspective, and style partake of imposed conventions to which his whim and wit must adapt themselves. To some readers this objectivity may appear mechanical and may also indicate a failing creativity in need of crutches. The likelihood, however, is that Cabell was in need not of crutches but of new styles of "learned sock"—in Milton's phrase—to insure changes of comic stance and pace from those in the "Biography."

Hamlet Had an Uncle is a retelling of the story of Hamlet as it existed before Shakespeare completely transformed it. Cabell's chief source is the English version of a *nouvelle* included in François de Belleforest's *Histoires tragiques,* published in Paris in 1576. From this *nouvelle*—scholars now agree—Hamlet got on the English stage. Whatever other sources Shakespeare may have used, he must have had Belleforest at hand, either in French or in English. In by-passing Shakespeare to get back to the Hamlet of Belleforest, Cabell decided that Belleforest's version of the story, while acceptable for the main characters and incidents, should be recast in the style of the Norse sagas from which Belleforest derived it but with whatever omissions, modifications, or elaborations appeared advisable in the light of this still earlier saga material.

In effect, then, Cabell also transforms Belleforest, but he does so in a way diametrically opposed to Shakespeare's. Shakespeare advances Hamlet into the sophisticated world of Renaissance tragedy, but Cabell returns him to the primitivistic world from which he originally came. Without in any way abrogating or mitigating this primitivism—compact of carnalities, atrocities, and insane conceptions of "face" or "honor"—he embellishes it and, paradoxically enough, with nuances borrowed from the more decadently sophisticated romances and tales of his own "Biography." The result is a brawling, leering comic chronicle about Hamlet and his associates that has no parallel anywhere in the world's literature, even amongst parodies of Shakespeare.

As the title in fact indicates, Hamlet's uncle—rather than Hamlet—is Cabell's protagonist. But the uncle in question is not the paternal one, Fengon, on whom Shakespeare based Claudius. This paternal uncle Cabell presents as Hamlet's real father, whereas his supposed or nominal father—slain by Fengon at the outset—is Hamlet's actual paternal uncle; as Cabell puts it: "In this pleasant vein of romantic irony, by killing his own father, did Hamlet avenge the death of his uncle."[12] Cabell's protagonist is a maternal uncle, one Wiglerus, merely a name in Belleforest and wholly ignored by Shakespeare. Wiglerus, as Cabell develops him, is another skeptically minded Jurgen who in the robust Norse atmosphere has preserved some of his youthful physical powers without having to coax them as a loan from Mother Sereda. Hamlet becomes this cool Wiglerus' hot antagonist for the love of the King of Deira's daughter, Alftruda, and

for the lust of the Amazon-like Hermetrude, Queen of Pictland.
Ultimately Wiglerus, when he succeeds to the throne of Denmark and thus becomes liege-lord of Hamlet (who is King of
Jutland after his successful revenge), must follow the same conceptions of "face" or "honor" that have so ridiculously governed
the behavior of Hamlet. His following them, however, is a mas-
terpiece of clever unscrupulousness abetted by Providence. Hamlet is disposed of; his death is appropriately revenged; and Wiglerus reigns complacently secure after his long, incredible involvement in Hamlet's affairs.

Two amusing minor features of *Hamlet Had an Uncle* are
worth mentioning. Since Horvendile is the name of the elder
Hamlet in the Belleforest *nouvelle,* Cabell felt obliged to retain
this name. At the same time he felt that his own Horvendile-
figure of the "Biography"—the diabolical contriver of the fantasy
—ought not to be absent. His solution is to introduce this figure
but to call him Orton. Of the Cabellian Horvendile's many disguises, this is the one best underscoring the point that a fiend
by any other name will smell as foul. Cabell also felt that, even
in a world so little concerned with culture in the humanistic
sense, a poet or skald must be present. So he provides one in
the character of the headsman Magnus, who composes elegies in
contrapuntal prose about his victims. Magnus' destiny, as Wiglerus indicates, is " 'to pursue murder for art's sake.' "[13]

The King Was in His Counting House is a retelling of the
story of Cosimo dei Medici and his family circle. Although Cabell
took most of his characters and incidents from standard histories
treating of the Medici, he decided that the most satisfactory literary use originally made of similar although not identical material was in such Jacobean melodramas as Middleton's *Women
Beware Women,* Webster's *The White Devil,* and Tourneur's
The Revenger's Tragedy. He would, therefore, follow these dram-
atists in their practice of inventing new names for characters and
places they had plagiarized out of the criminal carnival of Italian
history. But from their wildly free handling of the details of
this history and from their choice of the rhetoric-heavy verse-
play as medium, he would deviate sharply. He would stick closely
—although not slavishly—to the facts. He would be content with
a prose fiction unfolding briskly in a well-plotted sequence of
scenes. Out of his own "Biography," he would import the ironic,
tragi-comic theme of the minor poet as a changeling in conflict

with his time and yet ultimately victimized by it. The result is a pseudo-historical romance-novel of the Renaissance skillfully blending intrigue, farce, and allegory into a headier brew than Somerset Maugham was able to concoct a few years later in *Then and Now.*

Cabell's Ferdinand dei Vetori—his name for Cosimo dei Medici —ascends to the dukedom of San Marco or Florence and then to the kingship of Melphé or Tuscany. In accord with Machiavellian policy, he rids himself of his Huguenot prime-minister Carneschi —the architect of his ascent—in order to stand in with the Pope. He manipulates the lives of his sons to further the peace and prosperity of Melphé.

His putative son Cesario—really the bastard of Carneschi—is Cabell's protagonist. Disillusioned by the discovery that his sweetheart Hypolita is a nymphomaniac, Cesario turns to her more virtuous sister, Hermia. When his father has made him a cardinal with the prospects of eventual elevation to the papacy, Cesario cannot marry Hermia. But he refuses to serve his father's ambitions any further and escapes to Branlon with the Lord of the Forest—the reader's old friend Smith from "The Nightmare Has Triplets"—to practice as a minor poet. Ferdinand takes Hermia as his morganatic wife and appoints his surviving eldest son, Prince Lorenzo, as co-regent of Melphé in order to test his abilities as its future king. Lorenzo succumbs to all the wiles of the power-seeking Hypolita and marries her after the murders of their respective mates. The dying Ferdinand summons Cesario back from Branlon, informs him of his true origin, and beseeches him to save both Hermia and Melphé from the infamous Hypolita and her corrupted consort. Cesario accepts this grim responsibility and discharges it with the cool efficiency of a Wiglerus. Thus Melphé conquers Branlon in his loyalty, and Cesario becomes another Ferdinand.

The First Gentleman of America is a retelling of the story of Nemattanon, an Indian prince or werrowance of early Virginia's Ajacan, said to be the son of the god Quetzal and grandson of the White Cloud Serpent. Taking the name of Don Luis de Velasco from the viceroy of New Spain, Nemattanon learned the ways of the Spanish in Florida and Mexico and then visited Spain itself to receive honors from King Philip. Encouraged and aided by the historian A. J. Hanna, Cabell reconstructed Nemattanon's fantastic career from an extensive array of histories, antiquarian monographs, and original narratives, as well as from oral traditions furnished him by numerous collectors.

While pursuing his investigation, he even discovered in the junk room of the City Hall of St. Augustine, Florida, the chest-like coffin in which the remains of one of the chief figures in Nemattanon's story—his godfather, the Spanish leader Don Pedro Menéndez of Avilés, founder of St. Augustine—had been placed in 1574. When Don Pedro's remains were removed from this coffin in 1924 to be interred in an urn in the Cathedral of Avilés, a delegation of eminent citizens of Florida went overseas to bring back the coffin and a headboard from the tomb. A city fête commemorated their return with the relics. The headboard became an exhibition piece at Stetson University, but the coffin was relegated to the junk room and forgotten—until Cabell went poking about with the elevator man one Saturday afternoon in January, 1940.[14]

The materials he had thus gathered, Cabell decided, must be cast into a fictional form preserving the gambits and devices of folklore. Present sites must be identified with the ancient settings; variant legends must be reported; the poetry of full names and titles had to be preserved. It was imperative that the narration should reproduce the tone and the first-person intrusions of the collector of legend absorbed in all the curious ramifications of his subject. Cabell would take the liberty, however, to exploit—in the manner of the "Biography"—his hero's involvements in amour and dialectic as his Adamic innocence reacted to the gallantry and chivalry of the Spanish way of life. The result is one of the most subtly comic historical romances of Colonial America. The kind of conquest that put the glory of God and country above humane considerations—Cabell is blandly showing the reader—converted the recipients of its benefits all too completely to the doctrine that the end justifies the means.

Nemattanon undergoes a conflict of loyalties that centers more in his relations to his father Quetzal and his godfather Don Pedro than in his relations to his native wife, Leota, and to his several foreign mistresses. The fact that Don Pedro regards him as a kind of substitute for his own lost son and the fact that Quetzal is a renegade Spaniard hiding his real identity in the guise of an Indian tribal deity complicate the situation. For Nemattanon, Don Pedro comes to symbolize both the good and the evil of civilization. Quetzal, on the other hand, is the uncompromising upholder of cultural primitivism, of the good life as regression to "the Wild." Having a soft place in his heart for Don Pedro the man until the very end, Nemattanon learns from Don Pedro's cruelty as a Spanish leader, especially to the French, and from his fanaticism as a Catholic that Ajacan must resist the encroachment of civilization with treacheries and, if need be, atrocities. Returned to his tribe the young werrowance, shedding the urbanity of Don Luis de Velasco, follows Quetzal in regression and ultimately in hardness; then he vanishes into oblivion.

"Heirs and Assigns," despite the diversity of its parts in material and form, possesses the unity of an underlying ethical theme. In the case of each protagonist, the egoistic drive toward self-realization finally yields to the altruistic urge to do what he is expected to do in the place his society has made for him. Cabell puts it as follows: "The would-be nonconformist is compelled, by-and-by, to accept in this world his decreed heritage, whether as an heir or an assign; and he accepts likewise the requirements, the enforced requirements, of his heritage."[15] Wiglerus, the playboy of the northern world, succumbs to its code of "honor" when he becomes King of Denmark. Cesario, the poetic revolté against commonsense, assumes the role of a practical politician bent on saving and serving the Melphé to whose rule the law of succession—as well as its dying monarch—calls him. Nemattanon, after having his fling as Don Luis de Velasco, lives up to his obligations as the Werrowance of Ajacan.

The ultimate unity and value of this trilogy, however, go deeper. Issued between 1938 and 1943, with *The King Was in His Counting House* being first in order of composition and publication, "Heirs and Assigns" conceals beneath its sustained comic *élan* and its occasional impudent salacities Cabell's despairful brooding on the tragedy of politics in the long vista of human history. *Hamlet Had an Uncle* is a disillusioned exposé of Feudalism and its horrors; *The King Was in His Counting House* lays bare the hideousness of Renaissance Machiavellianism; *The First Gentleman of America* peers into the process of Europe's colonial expansion—the process that the historian Walter Prescott Webb has since so brilliantly illuminated in *The Great Frontier*—and discerns the sinister genies of Imperialism and Tribal Chauvinism. In the power politics of Totalitarianism's attempted *coup de monde* before and during the onset of World War II, Cabell must have been shudderingly aware of the recrudescence of all these spectres from man's political heritage. But, in giving vent to this awareness and to his cynicism concerning the role Democratic Idealism seemed to be playing a second time in the twentieth century, he characteristically avoided either directness or seriousness. What he most profoundly felt is not only veiled in flippancies and pedantries but also dissipated in the aesthetic zest of working with somewhat fresh materials and partially new forms.

Considered together, the ethical and political themes of the trilogy set against each other a melioristic view of the transformation of human selfishness and a pessimistic view of the eternal recurrence of man's inhumanity to man. Wiglerus, Cesario, and Nemattanon may exhibit some improvement in their personal conduct—relatively regarded—by becoming more altruistic, responsible, and conformist. But the dispensations to which they defer—absolutely regarded—remain diabolic. In these works of Cabell is a variation of Swift's, of Mark Twain's, of Reinhold Niebuhr's theme—"moral man and immoral society." Here, too, is a further twist, an extended dimension, of the Cabellian "comic waste."

IV *"It Happened in Florida"*

"It Happened in Florida" is the last of Cabell's trilogies to include fictions. The first volume, *The St. Johns: A Parade of Diversities,* is non-fictional, a contribution—done in collaboration with the historian A. J. Hanna—to The Rivers of America Series, which was under the general editorship of Stephen Vincent Benét and Carl Carmer. The second volume, *There Were Two Pirates: A Comedy of Division,* is a short romance about Spain, the high seas, and St. Augustine in the late eighteenth and early nineteenth century. The third volume, *The Devil's Own Dear Son: A Comedy of the Fatted Calf,* is a slightly longer romance-anatomy of St. Augustine in the 1920's and during the Cabells' residence there in the 1930's and thereafter. The main interest of this trilogy for the student of Cabell is that it represents his final attempt to expand and relate—in a context of fresh Floridian materials—the fluvial and the comedic metaphors that have been noted earlier as so important to his vision of human existence in the total scheme of the "Biography."

More than any other volume in The Rivers of America Series, *The St. Johns* supplies philosophical overtones and perspectives for the historical panorama of lives and events associated with the river. This is apparent in the opening chapter in the treatment of the prehistoric aborigines who called themselves Timucuans and of whom accurate knowledge is scant. What is said of them—and the prose is unmistakably Cabell's—applies to all the other characters who throng this incredible but true chronicle: "They existed; and for a little while this fact seemed, to them, of a noticeable importance, an importance which interested Heaven. Love (with an inadequate outcome) and decay and many vain regrets, and death too, went among them, like tyrants; and yet always hope remained, along with one's self-condonation, to whisper about a rather more just future and a much more superb tomorrow."[16]

The epilogue chapter not only sustains the philosophic note but also clinches the metaphorical significance of the river. In a sprightly dialogue, Cabell and Hanna review the results of their collaboration. One of Cabell's remarks is as follows: "Upon no other river in the United States have white men lived for so long a while, or so variously; and I choose to regard its history far less as a record of events, and of commerce, and of fruit raising, than as a pageant of strange persons passing, with Time as their drum major, beside its broad brown waters. Nor is it a monotonous pageant, this outlandish parade which, starting with the imperial swagger of Jean Ribaut, ends with a furtive, stumbling, and tipsy Cora McNeil."[17] It is notable that Cabell directs the reader's attention to a chivalrous explorer and to a decadently gallant courtesan and brothel-keeper who married the poet and novelist Stephen Crane as the initial and final bubbles on the stream.

To Hanna's last observation, "We have dealt, beyond doubt, with a somewhat motley squad of oddities," Cabell makes this closing reply: "Yes: for human nature is not merely undulant and diverse; it is also, as an acute philosopher has pointed out, a rum one. So with this aged moral, my dear friend, let us dismiss the grotesque and highly colored pageant which, as if under the influence of an enchantment just slightly sinister, has trooped toward us from out of our river's fantastic past, and which now evades us."[18] His is the voice of Prospero or Horvendile.

José Gasparilla, the pirate hero of *There Were Two Pirates*, and Diego de Arredondo Dodd, the tourist-home proprietor who is the protagonist of *The Devil's Own Dear Son*, lead lives very

much in accord with the basic scenario of Cabell's cosmic vaudeville—the dream of youth, the effort to realize this dream, and the
coming to terms with both Time's double-dealing and the dream's
inadequacy. Also, the *dramatis personae* of the first skit are
ancestors of those in the second since Gasparilla married the
widow of the Don Diego de Arredondo who was the father of
Diego Dodd's still-living great-aunt on his mother's side. Finally,
Gasparilla and Diego Dodd, by use of the same magic green
birthstone and on Walburga's Eves in their respective centuries,
become involved with the spectral essences and the infernal
presences subsisting timelessly in the mistiness of Time's restless
waters.

Gasparilla's narrative is in his own first-person. His mutiny,
piracies, murders, and adulteries—all committed in the cause or
course of accumulating enough wealth to live happily ever after
with the Isabel he has left behind in Spain—compose a memoir
having much of the sustained irony of Fielding's *Jonathan Wild*
and of Thackeray's *Barry Lyndon*. Boarding a ship whose loot he
thinks will complete the sum he has set himself, Gasparilla makes
the disillusioning discovery that his Isabel is married, has five
children, and is growing fat. Thereafter, he becomes a bit pathetic.
His recovery of his boyhood—through the aid of Isabel's husband,
the magic birthstone, and St. Augustine's Gates of Horn—constitutes a narrative in a wholly different style. Most of it is a
nine-year-old's simple, innocent, tender record of his family, his
aspirations, and his first love's onset.

Returning to St. Augustine, Gasparilla finds that his shadow—
from which he was magically divided when setting out for the
realm of essence—has been upholding and even enhancing his
criminal reputation. He also finds that Isabel is a widow with
an additional sixth child. He takes advantage of the situation
to provide Isabel's offspring with a new father and to turn
himself into a highly respected pillar of society and the church.
Telling anecdotes about his infamous relative, he lives comfortably on loot he has previously buried in places known only
to himself. Cabell's *Comedy of Division* is thus really a comedy
of reformation—a theme on which Cabell's own life had prepared him to be an authority.

The original draft of *The Devil's Own Dear Son* was in Diego
Dodd's first-person. But Cabell feared this confession style might
mislead readers into thinking he approved his protagonist's record

of thieveries, forgeries, perjuries, illicit amours, murders, falsification of income tax returns, and evasions of jury duty and the draft. So he recast the whole into the omniscient author third-person, with some use of the second-person and of indirect discourse to give the reader the illusion of identification with Diego's experience.[19]

Diego compiled his malodorous record while away from the Bide-A-While tourist home kept by his Dickensian parents. Returning home, he finds his mother long since dead, his father comfortably senescent, and St. Augustine with a tourist boom and augmented antiquities. Keeping silent about his past, Diego assumes charge of his father's business and soon becomes a pillar of society comparable to the reformed Gasparilla. He prepares to marry his now no longer young first love, Catherine Mary Zapo, about whom he once built a dream castle. The reader's friend Smith of "The Nightmare" had married her in Diego's long absence but has deserted her to dwell in Branlon.

Lest Diego should marry unaware of his potentiality for begetting red-headed changelings, his supposed father unveils the family skeleton. Diego was delivered to his mother down the chimney in a ball of fire. His real father is Red Samaël, Satan's eternally youthful, untiringly lecherous assistant devil. Before marrying Mrs. Catherine M. Smith, Diego decides to perform an act of filial piety. With Gasparilla's birthstone in his pocket, he goes through the city's Gates of Horn to find Red Samaël in Hell.

In *The Devil's Own Dear Son* is "the quest for the father" motif so ubiquitous in the modern novel. Here, also, is the prodigal son story given a new twist. When Diego finally reaches Red Samaël, this youthful father—after reviewing his middle-aged son's record—concludes that it is so feebly nefarious as to amount virtually to a betrayal of Hell's exacting immoral standards, a regrettable example of backsliding toward respectability. Though disappointed in Diego, Red Samaël is ready—so to speak —to kill the fatted calf for him by gratifying any and all of his desires with the consoling reminder that " 'it is never too late to relapse.' "[20]

The one desire that Diego would gratify is to revisit his dream castle in the realm of essence. Entering there by the devil's magic, he discovers that it is a dated, rococo improvisation, ill-suited to commonsense living. Its tenants are images of happiness, success, heroism, and iniquity conceived in a spirit of "high-pitched unhumorous innocence.' "[21] Red Samaël offers him opulence, power, even his lost youth back again, but Diego prefers a new heating installation in the Bide-A-While tourist home. He and his foster father and Mrs. Catherine Smith Dodd and their guests can then abide quite comfortably in the stable transience or transient stability characteristic of this kind of establishment. When his wish is granted, he throws into the sea the magic green stone. Cabell's *Comedy of the Fatted Calf* is thus really a comedy of security—that bourgeois fetish for which the aging human animal will forego his Faustian birthright of high incitements.

The diabolism Cabell has long associated with such high incitements and with his own creativity receives, in *The Devil's Own Dear Son*, a salutary exorcism. Hell is no longer what it used to be. In a mock-Miltonic "great consult" in Hell worthy of C. S. Lewis, Satan and his assistants agree on a new policy to relieve Hell's overcrowding. They will raise the admission requirements, encourage new applicants to seek other lodgings for the dead, send regular allotments of their own population to become displaced damned souls in outer space, and even propagandize on earth to promote an upturn in ascensions to Jehovah's Heaven. Cabell's subtitle might also have been, then, "A Comedy of Damnation."

As an anatomy, this last fiction in the Cabellian canon is sufficiently wide-glancing to include the book clubs, the writers they assist to popularity, and the criticism that for so long has sought to bury Cabell and all his works. As a book-club subscriber, the now respectable Diego is an authority on the merits of such geniuses as Francis X. Flubberdub, Gideon Gibberish, Natalie Babu English, and Laura Caconym Nugatory. From the picturesque assortment of legendary horses under the care of the fiendish herdsman Asmodeus, Diego chooses the silver stallion of Poictesme. Asmodeus tells him he has picked what " 'is nowadays an infirm and discredited animal' " and goes on to explain: " 'He has seen much service; and between ourselves, those veterinarians whose opinions as to aesthetic matters are just at present viewed seriously, tell me that he is ill-constructed and weak-knee'd, in addition to having been overridden.' "[22]

Diego's mount of course heads homeward for the Cabellian countries of the imagination, and Diego is content to proceed toward Hell by this roundabout and infrequently traveled route. He is impressed by these countries' "unmoral latitude and benign coloring"; but, when later "asked about present-day conditions" there, he must regretfully admit that "there was not any up-to-date or really complete summary to be had anywhere."[23] It is to be hoped that the present study will to some extent remedy this lack. If one employed a subtitle on the title page, it might very well read: *James Branch Cabell: A Comedy of Incorrigibility.*

CHAPTER 7

Final Judgment

THE ASSUMPTION with which this critical-analytical study began—that Cabell's work possesses complexity—should have emerged from the detailed evidence of the preceding chapters as established beyond argument. His is a copious many-sidedness that defies pat categorization, rebuffs simplistic critical formulae, and proves hospitable only to an informed catholic taste. The carpers who have imputed to him nothing more than an unduly prolonged and fecund preoccupation with flight, frippery, and fornication should forever hold their peace.

The "Biography" alone—despite faults that have been unsparingly pointed out—is the achievement of a mind and art labyrinthinely involved with accretions and continuities of tradition and with dilemmas and adventures of modernity. This eighteen-volume opus extends southern regionalism into a fourth allegorical dimension; it sets the "nothing but" of reductive naturalism over against the "as if" of pragmatic faith; it revives and reconstitutes the comic spirit; it flouts the novel through experiments with other forms of prose fiction. Both structurally and stylistically, it qualifies for a prominent place within the twentieth century's vivid and beautiful axis of the arts.

The considerable body of writing Cabell did after the "Biography" also has a complexity of its own. The mind and art of the earlier work persist in it as diversely in touch as ever with the human and aesthetic past and present, but Cabell was willing to risk new soundings and directions to the very end.

How coherent are the components of the Cabellian complexity? How fraught are they with permanent human significance? These basic questions were originally posed to be answered. As phrased, they may have for admirers of Cabell an alien smack of the graduate seminar and the coterie quarterly. But the criteria they invoke are surely implicit in the touchstones of John Charteris in *Beyond Life:* "Off-hand . . . I would say that books are best insured against oblivion through practice of the auctorial virtues of distinction and clarity, of beauty and symmetry, of tenderness and truth and urbanity."[1]

Purely formal coherence is marked in the smaller and largest units of Cabell's work—the sentence, paragraph, chapter, tale, and essay on the one hand, and the cycle and trilogy on the other. But often the individual book is less formally coherent. It tends to be made up of episodes and, as a totality, to be itself merely an episode in a more comprehensive design. *Figures of Earth* and *Jurgen* are cases in point, as are most of the other major romances of the "Biography" and also some of the books in the later trilogies.

This curious ambivalent looseness in book after book—a continuous dissolving of its integrity, as one reads, into either a brilliant discreet diversity or the vague portent of an encompassing supra-unity—can be bewildering as well as fascinating. The clarities of successive chapters produce an aggregate obscurity that only the next book in the sequence will clarify—but with such a repetition of the process that the reader is left looking for final clarification.

Modern fiction, of course, abounds in cycles, tetralogies, and trilogies: the sequence-novel or the *roman fleuve* has flowed too steadily, too abundantly since Balzac. But in most of them the individual book, particularly the novel as opposed to the collection of short stories, is less episodic, more tightly unified, than is the case with Cabell's major fictions. The fact that the latter are not novels at all but blends of the other forms of prose fiction—the romance, the anatomy, and the confession—accounts for the anomaly.

Coherence between content and form in Cabell is impressive, especially in two respects. His sportively dualistic skepticism, soaring into dream or swooping toward negation, finds fit expression in a prose of ecstasies and quips, elegancies and colloquialisms, sonorities and snickers. The genre best accommodated to this skepticism and its pliant, medley prose is the hybrid one of the romance-anatomy, since dream or its equivalent is the stuff of the romance, and satire is virtually the anatomy's synonym. The comic spirit at its gayest, its most ironic, and its most indiscreet can caper and sprawl uninhibited in the double bed thus provided. In the case of a writer with Cabell's education, some elements of the confession are inseparable from such a context.

Does the quality of Cabell's satire suffer from his Janus-faced skepticism? Are allegory and this kind of skepticism entirely congenial? The convictions prompting these questions may be stated as follows: (1) unless satire has fixed ethical norms, it dissipates itself into breezy and perverse derision; (2) unless allegory rests on a systematic faith, with its interlocking ontological, cosmological, and other doctrines, it turns into an animation of random abstractions wantoning in a void or posturing amidst chaos.

Some incoherence due to the causes here suggested mars Cabell's comedy and the countries of his imagination. The way of poetry, as he conceives it, does provide norms for satire. But the artist's individualism and creativity, though potent and admirable rods to chasten and subdue some of mankind's follies, cowardices, and manias, verge so much and so often on the highfalutin and erratic—and are so committed to an economy of extremism—that they weaken satire's cutting edge and blur its ends of sanity and love of the good. Here is where gallantry and chivalry at their best might provide saving norms of sweet reasonableness and grace—and Cabell does deploy them for this purpose, but not with sufficient consistency or frequency to clear away all confusion and ambiguity.

Cabell's *volte-face* skepticism makes for too much latitude and license not only in the geographies and mythologies of his fictive worlds, but also in the ideological shenanigans that he performs in them with his endless supply of slightly differing puppets from the same old stockroom. These abstract and glittering manikins are often superbly lively. The chivalrous, gallant, poetic, or diabolic composition and destiny of many of them are clear and cogent. Their thronged and colorful stage, amply furnished with antiques of many periods, is scarcely a void. But sometimes it is a bit chaotic, and the supporting abstractions on display in this or that alcove of the mausoleum seem to have been placed there at random. As a mode, allegory can trap itself into baffling complications; and this hazard is sometimes unavoidable when the mind of the allegorist likes to dart—as Cabell's does—from one philosophic position to another. But perhaps Edmund Wilson is right in implying that what plays the devil with allegory may be a state of grace for dream comedy.[2]

The permanent human significance of Cabell's complexity is real but special. Because he is not writing novels, he cannot fully satisfy most readers' demand for character in society—so presented as to afford them the psychological insights, the empathies, and the catharses that illuminate their day-to-day experiences and permit them to share in those that others are undergoing or have undergone. But if such readers will pay attention to the elaborate anticness of his extensive Punch-and-Judy show, they may find themselves doing what they have seldom done before—looking down the long vista of their own and others' experiences and seeing in this stream of time the hidden essences and forces with which they had always been dimly familiar but never so amusedly, bemusedly, and vividly concerned as now. One eventually comes to realize that this is not an ordinary entertainment or escape but a rare kind of serio-comic necromancy that only a Puckish genealogist suckled on outworn creeds but blessed with a nimble brain, a sensitive heart, and an incredible vocabulary could ever have devised.

What may most annoy one at first with Cabell is an apparent central discrepancy at the heart of much that he has done. He insists that "man alone of animals plays the ape to his dreams." But his attempts in the "Biography" and in the later writings to make his readers grasp this genuinely tender and urbane primary truth usually center on personae of all genders whose past or present conduct is evidence that the phrase "of animals" is the most important item in the formulation—or, in other words, that man remains pretty much of an ape in essence. And often Cabell seems to assume that this secondary and appalling truth is merrier or funnier even than the primary one—is, indeed, the real cream of the jest.

On second thought, one may conclude that here is merely the inevitable consequence of his being a kind of neo-romantic comedian or comedist in an age of naturalism. But such an historical palliation begs the critical question as to whether the seeming central discrepancy in his conception and portrayal of mankind from Manuel to Diego Dodd is an unpardonable aesthetic and ethical flaw, or an additional credit to his distinction as an ironist.

Final Judgment

On still further thought, one may decide that no ready answer to this conundrum is possible. Man began his long pilgrimage from the cave to the fallout shelter with acts of vice and folly, of crime, and of sex for sex's sake; he has persisted in such irrationalities throughout his known history; he has shown his capacity for them on a grander scale already in the twentieth century than in any previous span of years; and he will doubtless terminate his existence by adding to the record more of the same before and during the holocaust that now—all authorities assert—waits only on time and temperament. In view of these simple facts of life, is it fair to condemn Cabell for not blinking the presence of the beasts in the jungle, the little hut, and the river, and yet finding a way of regarding them that, for him at least, kept horror and hate from making mincemeat out of serenity and love?

The trend of these remarks is toward an inevitable conclusion. Whether one likes or dislikes Cabell, whether or not one finds him re-readable or, for that matter, even readable at all, one must—in common decency and simple justice—rank him among the major rather than the minor authors of the twentieth century —and in a world perspective rather than merely an American or an Anglo-American one. He belongs, not with the Edgar Saltuses and Ronald Firbanks, the Thorne Smiths and Robert A. Heinleins—as good as most of these sometimes are—but with such many-faceted supranational men of letters as Bernard Shaw and André Gide. Cabell is both the Spenser and the Boccaccio of the second American Renaissance.[3]

Notes and References

Preface

1. Cabell, *Works* (Storisende ed.), XVIII, 319-44, provides a list of his magazine pieces and their uses in his books to 1930.

2. Cabell, *Works*, VII, p. xv; or *Preface to the Past*, p. 110.

3. Cabell, *Works*, XVII, 282-86, quotes from representative newspaper notices of *The Line of Love* and its immediate successors.

4. For a brief discussion of this movement in relation to succeeding trends, see Joe Lee Davis, "The American Writer and the Nobel Prize," *Michigan Alumnus Quarterly Review*, LXII (Autumn, 1955), 23-55.

5. Lewis, *The Man from Main Street*, ed. by H. E. Maule and M. H. Cane (New York, 1953), pp. 8, 16-17.

6. Cabell, *Preface to the Past*, p. 48, and *Works*, XVII, 9-10, 293-97.

7. In the epilogue (dated May, 1921) of *The Lineage of Lichfield;* Cabell, *Works*, XVI, 291-98.

8. Paul Elmer More, *The Demon of the Absolute*, New Shelburne Essays, I (Princeton, 1928), pp. 58-62; Granville Hicks, *The Great Tradition* (New York, 1933), pp. 220-21; and Alfred Kazin, *On Native Grounds* (New York, 1942), pp. 227-35, represent, respectively, the three views of Cabell referred to in this paragraph.

9. See Virginia J. Rock, *The Making and Meaning of I'll Take My Stand: A Study in Utopian-Conservatism, 1925-1939* (University of Minnesota, unpublished Ph.D. dissertation, 1961).

10. Their re-evaluations are listed and annotated in the Selected Bibliography of the present volume, under Secondary Sources.

11. By Peter Monro Jack, *New Republic*, LXXXIX (Jan. 13, 1937), 323-26.

12. Thorp, *American Writing in the Twentieth Century* (Cambridge, Mass., 1960), pp. 53-54.

13. Fishwick, *The Virginia Tradition* (Washington, D.C., 1956), p. 46. In his *Virginia: A New Look at the Old Dominion* (New York, 1959), pp. 184-95, he somewhat modifies his earlier view.

14. Beach, *The Outlook for American Prose* (Chicago, 1926), pp. 63-80, and *The Twentieth Century Novel: Studies in Technique* (New York, 1932), pp. 85-93; Guérard, *Literature and Society* (New York, 1935) and *Art for Art's Sake* (*idem*, 1936), *passim;* Van Doren, *The American Novel, 1789-1939* (New York, 1940), pp. 315-22. For

Notes and References

Van Doren's book-length study of Cabell and for Parrington, Howard, and Wilson, see Selected Bibliography of the present volume, under Secondary Sources.

15. Cabell, *Special Delivery*, p. 40.

Chapter One

1. Cabell, *Ladies and Gentlemen*, p. 252.
2. Cabell, *Let Me Lie*, p. 163.
3. Cabell, *Ladies and Gentlemen*, pp. 252-53.
4. Cabell, *Let Me Lie*, p. 155.
5. Cabell, *As I Remember It*, p. 152.
6. Robert Beverley Munford, Jr., *Richmond Homes and Memories* (Richmond, 1936), pp. 118-19. William Manchester, *Disturber of the Peace* (New York, 1951), pp. 225-26, and Edgar Kemler, *The Irreverent Mr. Mencken* (Boston, 1950), p. 258, comment on Mencken's efforts in behalf of the nomination of Ritchie, respectively, in 1928 and 1932.
7. Munford, pp. 159-60, 10.
8. Cabell, *Let Me Lie*, pp. 181-99.
9. *Ibid.*, pp. 143-59.
10. *Ibid.*, pp. 154-58.
11. *Ibid.*, pp. 147-48.
12. *Ibid.*, pp. 148-49, 154-56.
13. Glasgow, *The Woman Within* (New York, 1954), pp. 130-32.
14. *Ibid.*, pp. 133-34. Cabell, *Some of Us*, pp. 47-58; *Let Me Lie*, pp. 231-67; and *As I Remember It*, pp. 217-33, discusses Ellen Glasgow. In the last of these references, pp. 217-18, he generally questions the factual accuracy of her handling in *The Woman Within* of all matters involving him, but does not specify or explain. Emmett B. Peter, Jr., "Cabell: The Making of a Rebel," *Carolina Quarterly*, XIV (Spring, 1962), 74-81, sets straight the facts of the Williamsburg and Richmond scandals.
15. Glasgow, pp. 133-34; Peter, p. 79.
16. Cabell, *Special Delivery*, p. 23; Peter, p. 79.
17. Glasgow, pp. 134-35. See note 14, *supra*. Cabell, *Works*, XIV, 5-6, makes fictional use of this murder mystery, with interesting variations in the details confirming Peter's correction of Glasgow.
18. Cabell, *Works*, XI, 9-30, develops his theory of fiction concerned with "beautiful happenings."
19. Cabell, *Preface to the Past*, pp. 32-34, or *Works*, XVI, 254-56.
20. Cabell, *Ladies and Gentlemen*, pp. 221-23.
21. Cf. Frederic I. Carpenter, *American Literature and the Dream* (New York, 1955), pp. 130-32, on the Devil in Emerson *et al.*

22. Cabell, *Preface to the Past*, pp. 30, 129-31, and *Works*, XVI, 252, and IX, pp. xv-xvii. John Philips Cranwell and James P. Cover, *Notes on Figures of Earth* (New York, 1929), pp. 23-24, discuss Horvendile's genesis; Harvey Wickham, *The Impuritans* (New York, 1929), pp. 148-49, quips interestingly about his name and role.

23. Cabell, *As I Remember It*, pp. 199-201, advances the theory that the afflatus of the sincere writer is more diabolic than divine; *Works*, XVII, 268, plays with the idea of his imp or daemon.

24. Cabell, *Ladies and Gentlemen*, pp. 213-25.

25. *Ibid.*, p. 225.

26. This and the preceding paragraph are based on Cabell, *Preface to the Past*, pp. 83-89, or *Works*, V, pp. xi-xv.

27. Both *The Line of Love* and *Gallantry* are introduced by dedicatory epistles to Mrs. Grundy; Cabell, *Works*, VII, 3-6, and IX, pp. xxv-xxix.

28. Several unwritten books attributed to Stevenson as well as nonexistent works by imaginary authors created by Butler, Hewlett, and Machen are in John Charteris' library at Willoughby Hall in *Beyond Life;* see Cabell, *Works*, I, 9-10. Cabell, *Special Delivery*, pp. 25-26, pays tribute to *Esmond.*

29. Cabell, *Works*, X, 3-4.

30. Cabell, *Special Delivery*, pp. 132-36, 134.

31. This description is based on illustrations and details in Percival Reniers, *The Springs of Virginia: Life, Love, and Death at the Waters, 1775-1900* (Chapel Hill, N.C., 1941), as well as on Cabell, *These Restless Heads*, pp. 62-65.

32. Reniers, pp. 82, 281-82.

33. *Ibid.*, pp. 362-63, and Cabell, *These Restless Heads*, pp. 59-60.

34. Quoted by Reniers, p. 263.

35. Cabell, *These Restless Heads*, pp. 60-61.

36. *Ibid.*, p. 60.

37. *Ibid.*, pp. 65-68.

38. Keith Thomas, "The Double Standard," *Journal of the History of Ideas* XX (April, 1959), 195-216, provides the best discussion.

39. This paragraph is based primarily on Cabell, *Quiet, Please*, pp. 79-105.

40. Cabell, *As I Remember It*, pp. 3-7, 16-17.

41. *Ibid.*, pp. 8, 42-43, lists some of Priscilla's fictional derivatives.

42. *Ibid.*, pp. 23-25.

43. Van Vechten, *Fragments from an Unwritten Autobiography*, 2 vols. (New Haven, 1955), I, 33-34.

44. Cabell, *As I Remember It*, pp. 17-18.

45. *Ibid.*, pp. 55.

46. *Ibid.*, pp. 29-34.

47. *Ibid.*, pp. 45-55.

48. *Ibid.,* pp. 83-85.
49. *Ibid.,* pp. 39-40.
50. *Ibid.,* pp. 62-63, 69.
51. *Ibid.,* pp. 56-61, 63-68.
52. *Ibid.,* pp. 183-89, discusses Holt's influence; see also Cabell, *Works,* I, pp. xv-xvi, or *Preface to the Past,* pp. 23-24.
53. Cabell, *Ladies and Gentlemen,* pp. 19-20, 300, 303-4, links the two works on this basis.
54. See Joe Lee Davis, "The Case for Comedy in Caroline Theatrical Apologetics," *PMLA,* LVIII (June, 1943), 353-71, for detailed anatomizing of this Puritan practice.
55. Cabell, *Works,* I, p. xiv, or *Preface to the Past,* p. 22.
56. See Robert H. Elias, *Theodore Dreiser: Apostle of Nature* (New York, 1949), pp. 113-16, 193-94, for discussion of the Doubleday and John Lane episodes respectively.
57. Cabell, *Works,* XVIII, 269-324, includes *Jurgen and the Law,* ed. Guy Holt. Statements in this and subsequent paragraphs about the *Jurgen* case, except for Van Vechten's role, are based on this source.
58. Van Vechten, I, 26-27.
59. Cabell, *Works,* XVIII, 252, or *Preface to the Past,* p. 266.
60. Statements in this paragraph are based on Emily Clark, *Innocence Abroad* (New York, 1931), pp. 35-52, and on Cabell, *Let Me Lie,* pp. 203-28.
61. Rascoe, *Before I Forget* (New York, 1937), pp. 349-54, 386-95.
62. Hergesheimer, "James Branch Cabell," *The American Mercury,* XIII (January, 1928), 38-47.
63. DeCasseres' extravagant epigrammatic eulogy of him is cited on the jacket of the Signet paperback reprint of *Jurgen.*
64. Cabell, *As I Remember It,* pp. 189-94, 166-71, and 173-78, reviews his relations with these three respectively.
65. Cabell, *Some of Us,* p. 6, commends Davis', Pruette's and Kronenberger's fictions.
66. These all died in the fullness of their powers in 1928. Cabell, *Some of Us,* pp. 15-26, 29-39, pays tribute respectively to Newman and Wylie; *Works,* XVII, 47-53, and *Let Me Lie,* pp. 203-28, to Byrne.
67. Statements in this paragraph are based on Cabell, *As I Remember It,* pp. 71-77.
68. Cabell, *These Restless Heads,* pp. 27-32, 76-81; *Special Delivery, passim; Quiet, Please,* pp. 14-16; and *As I Remember It,* pp. 237-38.
69. Cabell, *As I Remember It,* pp. 205-16, reviews his relations with Benét and Hanna; pp. 96, 159, refers to the Rawlings friendship.
70. *Ibid.,* pp. 96-111.
71. *Ibid.,* pp. 125-31.

Chapter Two

1. Cabell, *Works*, XVIII, 241; *Preface to the Past*, p. 245.
2. Cabell, *Preface to the Past*, p. 28.
3. Cabell, *Works*, XVI, 251; *Preface to the Past*, p. 29.
4. Cabell, *Preface to the Past*, p. 28.
5. *Ibid.*, p. 104, *Works*, VII, p. x.
6. Cabell, *Preface to the Past*, p. 105; *Works*, VII, p. x, has "direct" for "final."
7. Cabell, *Preface to the Past*, pp. 105-6; *Works*, VII, p. xi.
8. Cabell, *Preface to the Past*, p. 106; *Works*, VII, p. xi.
9. *Ibid.*
10. *Ibid.*
11. Cabell, *Preface to the Past*, p. 106; *Works*, VII, p. xii.
12. Cabell, *Preface to the Past*, p. 107; *Works*, VII, p. xii.
13. Cabell, *Some of Us*, p. 86.
14. *Selected Writings and Speeches of Abraham Lincoln*, ed. T. Harry Williams (Chicago, 1943), p. 261.
15. Page's "The Burial of the Guns," Jewett's "The Hiltons' Holiday," Freeman's "The Revolt of Mother," and Harte's "Tennessee's Partner" illustrate these points.
16. Opie Read's *A Kentucky Colonel* (1890), *A Tennessee Judge* (1893), and *An Arkansas Planter* (1896) deserve reprinting in an omnibus.
17. Glasgow, *A Certain Measure* (New York, 1943), pp. 3-4.
18. Louis D. Rubin, Jr., *No Place on Earth: Ellen Glasgow, James Branch Cabell And Richmond-in-Virginia* (Austin, Texas, 1959), p. 67.
19. See Carl Van Vechten, *Fragments*, I, 35.
20. Cabell, *Works*, I, pp. ix-x; slightly expanded in *Preface to the Past*, pp. 15-16.
21. Cabell, *Works*, I, 36-38, 59.
22. See Stevens, "Another Weeping Woman," in *Harmonium* (New York, 1923), p. 42; *The Collected Poems* (New York, 1954), p. 25.
23. See Arthur O. Lovejoy, "The Thirteen Pragmatisms," *Journal of Philosophy, Psychology and Scientific Methods*, V (1908), Part I, 5-12; Part II, 29-39.
24. Cf. Edgar Sheffield Brightman, *Nature and Values* (New York, 1945), p. 33, and Morris R. Cohen, *Reason and Nature: An Essay on the Meaning of Scientific Method* (New York, 1931), pp. 450-57, 57-75.
25. Jules de Gaultier, *Le Bovarysme* (Paris, 1902) and *La Fiction universelle* (*idem*: 1903); Wilmot E. Ellis, *Bovarysm: The Art-Phi-*

losophy of Jules de Gaultier, University of Washington Chapbooks, No. 16 (Seattle, Washington, 1928).

26. My phrasing here in indebted to Cabell, *Some of Us,* p. 126, and Wagenknecht, *Cavalcade of the American Novel,* p. 253.

27. Cabell, *Works,* I, pp. xi, x.

28. Cabell, *Quiet, Please,* pp. 9-10.

29. Cabell, *Works,* I, 269.

30. *Ibid.,* p. 270.

31. Cf. Cabell, *Some of Us,* pp. 95-97, and *Works,* XVI, 291-98.

32. DeCasseres, *Chameleon: Being the Book of My Selves* (New York, 1922), p. 86. The best treatment of Cabell's development of the comic spirit is Arvin R. Wells, *Jesting Moses: A Study in Cabellian Comedy* (University of Michigan, unpublished Ph.D. dissertation, 1959).

33. Julia Cluck, "Elinor Wylie's Shelley Obsession," *PMLA,* LVI (September, 1941), 841-60.

34. Bradley *Shakespearean Tragedy* (New York, 1960), p. 29.

35. Cabell, *Works,* XVI, 258.

36. Cabell, *Works,* I, 35.

37. Frye, *Anatomy of Criticism: Four Essays* (Princeton, 1957), p. 304.

38. Henry James, *The Future of the Novel: Essays on the Art of Fiction,* ed. Leon Edel (New York, 1956), p. 14.

39. Kenyon, *The Golden Feather* (New York, 1943), p. vii.

40. Hersey, "The Novel of Contemporary History," *The Atlantic Monthly,* CLXXXIV (November, 1939), 80-84.

41. Frye, p. 304-6.

42. *Ibid.,* p. 314.

43. *Ibid.,* p. 313.

44. Cranwell and Cover, *Notes on Figures of Earth,* pp. 116-28.

45. Cabell, *Works,* I, 205.

46. *Ibid.,* pp. 201, 202, cites this work.

47. Cabell, *Some of Us,* pp. 20-22.

48. Cabell, *Smire,* p. 293.

49. *Ibid.,* p. 192.

50. *Ibid.,* pp. 291-95.

51. Cabell, *Works,* I, 247.

52. Cabell, *Smirt,* p. 284.

53. See Joe Lee Davis, "Criticism and Parody," *Thought,* XXVI (Summer, 1951), 180-204.

54. Frye, p. 34.

55. Cabell, *The Witch-Woman,* p. 13.

56. Frye, *loc. cit.*

57. Cf. Angus Wilson, *Emile Zola: An Introductory Study of his Novels* (New York, 1952), p. 60, and Helmut A. Hatzfeld, *Literature*

Through Art: A New Approach to French Literature (New York, 1952), p. 173 and *passim*.

58. E. M. Forster, *Aspects of the Novel* (New York, 1927), pp. 118-19, takes issue with Percy Lubbock's Jamesian *The Craft of Fiction* on the central importance of "point of view" in fictional method.

59. Warren A. McNeill, *Cabellian Harmonics*, (New York, 1928), pp. 33-82.

60. John Peale Bishop, "The Modernism of Mr. Cabell," in *The Collected Essays of John Peale Bishop*, ed. Edmund Wilson (New York, 1948), p. 242.

61. Cabell, *Works*, II, 124-26; Cranwell and Cover, pp. 50-54.

62. McNeill, pp. 13-19.

Chapter Three

1. Cabell, *Works*, II, 137.
2. *Ibid.*, p. 291.
3. *Ibid.*, p. 6.
4. *Ibid.*, pp. 292, 8.
5. *Ibid.*, p. x; *Preface to the Past*, p. 42.
6. Cabell, *Works*, II, 288.
7. *Ibid.*, p. 181.
8. Cabell, *Works*, III, 56: Miramon Lluagor tells how Manuel's keeping quiet earned him a reputation for wisdom and resourcefulness; Miramon's exclamation—" 'Keep mum with Manuel!' "—is an allusion to the slogan, "Keep cool with Coolidge."
9. Cabell, *Works*, XIV, 129.
10. *Ibid.*, pp. 124, 170.
11. *Ibid.*, p. 37.
12. *Ibid.*, p. 256.
13. *Ibid.*, p. 146.
14. *Ibid.*, pp. 180-81.
15. *Ibid.*, pp. 274, 20, 319.
16. Cabell, *Some of Us*, p. 95.

Chapter Four

1. The tale is reprinted in *The Smart Set Anthology*, ed. by Burton Rascoe and Groff Conklin (New York, 1934), pp. 182-95.
2. Cabell, *Preface to the Past*, pp. 254-62, includes the full text of the letter.
3. Cabell, *Works*, VI, 149, 136, 82.
4. *Ibid.*, p. 135.

5. *Ibid.,* pp. 323, 158-59.
6. *Ibid.,* p. 97.
7. *Ibid.,* pp. 152, 157.
8. *Ibid.,* p. 104.
9. *Ibid.,* pp. 173, 183.
10. *Ibid.,* p. 206.
11. *Ibid.,* p. 319.
12. *Ibid.,* pp. 278, 287, 288.
13. Cabell, *Works,* VIII, p. xv; *Preface to the Past,* p. 119.
14. Cabell, *Works,* VIII, 163-64.
15. Cabell, *Works,* VI, 309.
16. Cabell, *Works,* XVIII, 239-42, and *Preface to the Past,* pp. 243-46, tells how his difficulty with Tunbridge Wells—an actual setting he did not know—led him to invent Poictesme.
17. Cabell, *Works,* IX, 340.
18. *Ibid.,* pp. xi-xv; *Preface to the Past,* pp. 125-29.
19. Cabell, *Works,* IX, p. xi, and *Preface to the Past,* p. 125.
20. Cabell, *Works,* XII, p. xvi; *Preface to the Past,* p. 165.
21. Cabell, *Preface to the Past,* p. 106.
22. Cabell, *Works,* XIII, 257, 262-63.

Chapter Five

1. Cabell, *Works,* IV, 271.
2. *Ibid.,* p. 276.
3. Quotations in this paragraph are from Cabell, *Works,* VII, 278, 268.
4. Quotations in this paragraph are from *ibid.,* pp. 275, 276, 278.
5. Cabell, *Works,* X, 8-9: the epigram is Gerald's.
6. *Ibid.,* p. 311; the phrase is Gerald's.
7. *Ibid.,* p. 86.
8. *Ibid.,* p. 193.
9. *Ibid.,* p. 308.
10. *Ibid.,* p. xvi. Cabell, *Preface to the Past,* pp. 142-43, revised the last phrase to read "with the most liberal allotment of ease and pleasure."
11. Cabell, *Works,* XI, 109.
12. Quotations in this paragraph are from *ibid.,* pp. 277, 282, 283.
13. Quotations in this paragraph are from *ibid.,* pp. 183, 186.
14. Quotations in this paragraph are from Cabell, *Works,* XV, 4-8.
15. *Ibid.,* p. 32.
16. Quotations in this paragraph are from *ibid.,* pp. 230, 231, 210.
17. *Ibid.,* p. 49.

18. Quotations in this paragraph are from *ibid.*, pp. 50, 49, 52, 54-55.

19. *Ibid.*, pp. 127-28.

20. Quotations in this paragraph are from *ibid.*, pp. 21, 155, 157.

21. Quotations in this paragraph are from *ibid.*, pp. 178, 173.

22. Cabell, *Works*, XVI, 212.

23. Oscar Wilde, *The Picture of Dorian Gray* (New York, 1931), pp. 140-41.

24. Edd Winfield Parks, "Cabell's *Cream of the Jest*," *Modern Fiction Studies*, II (May, 1956), 68-70, discusses this device.

25. Robert F. Haugh, *Joseph Conrad: Discovery in Design* (Norman, Okla., 1957), pp. v, 88-101, discusses *"progression d'effet"* and examines it in *Chance.* E. K. Brown, *Rhythm in the Novel* (Toronto, 1950), *passim,* comments on these devices in *Howards End* and other Forster novels.

Chapter Six

1. Cabell, *The Devil's Own Dear Son,* p. 103.

2. Cabell, *Some of Us,* pp. 72-73, 110, 122, 129-31.

3. *Ibid.*, p. 43.

4. Cabell, *Special Delivery,* pp. 177, 180, 185.

5. This dictum from Poe's "The Quacks of Helicon—A Satire," *The Complete Tales and Poems of Edgar Allan Poe* (New York, 1938), p. 576, is also cited by Andrew Lang, *Letters to Dead Authors* (New York, 1886), p. 142.

6. Cabell, *Ladies and Gentlemen,* p. 245.

7. Wilson, "The James Branch Cabell Case Reopened," *The New Yorker* (April 21, 1956), p. 155.

8. Cabell, *Quiet, Please,* p. 68.

9. Cf. Cabell, *Smirt,* p. 284, with Hicks, *The Great Tradition* (ed. cit.), p. 221.

10. Cabell, *Smire,* p. 218.

11. Cabell, *Smirt,* p. 22.

12. Cabell, *Hamlet Had an Uncle,* p. 116.

13. *Ibid.*, p. 227.

14. Cabell, *The First Gentleman of America,* pp. 290-93.

15. Cabell, *Let Me Lie,* p. 99.

16. Cabell and Hanna, *The St. Johns,* p. 7.

17. *Ibid.*, p. 302.

18. *Ibid.*, p. 303.

19. Cabell, *The Devil's Own Dear Son,* p. xi.

20. *Ibid.*, p. 149.

21. *Ibid.*, p. 175: Diego's phrase.

22. *Ibid.*, p. 118.

23. *Ibid.*, p. 124.

Chapter Seven

1. Cabell, *Works,* I, 19.
2. Wilson, p. 150.
3. Frederick J. Hoffman, *The Modern Novel in America, 1900-1950* (Chicago, 1951), p. 117, links Cabell with a tradition originated in the United States by Edgar Saltus. Robert A. Heinlein's *Stranger in a Strange Land* (1961) is blurbed on its jacket as "Cabellesque." Edd Winfield Parks, "James Branch Cabell," in *Southern Renascence,* ed. by Louis D. Rubin, Jr., and Robert D. Jacobs (Baltimore, 1953), p. 251, puts Cabell's "Biography" in the tradition of Boccaccio's *Decameron* and *Genealogy of the Gentile Gods.*

Selected Bibliography

PRIMARY SOURCES

(Limited to the Works of Cabell Discussed in This Study.)

A. "Biography of the Life of Manuel"

The Works of James Branch Cabell, Storisende Edition, 18 vols. New York: Robert M. McBride & Company, 1927-1930:

I. *Beyond Life: Dizain des Démiurges* (pub. 1919).

II. *Figures of Earth: A Comedy of Appearances* (pub. 1912).

III. *The Silver Stallion: A Comedy of Redemption* (pub. 1926).

IV. *Domnei* (pub. as *The Soul of Melicent* 1913, rev. 1920) and *The Music from Behind the Moon* (1926): *Two Comedies of Woman-Worship.*

V. *Chivalry: Dizain des Reines* (pub. 1909, rev. 1921).

VI. *Jurgen: A Comedy of Justice* (pub. 1919).

VII. *The Line of Love: Dizain des Mariages* (pub. 1905, rev. 1921).

VIII. *The High Place: A Comedy of Disenchantment* (pub. 1923).

IX. *Gallantry: Dizain des Fêtes Galantes* (pub. 1907, rev. 1922).

X. *Something About Eve: A Comedy of Fig-Leaves* (pub. 1927).

XI. *The Certain Hour: Dizain des Poètes* (pub. 1916).

XII. *The Cords of Vanity: A Comedy of Shirking* (pub. 1909, rev. 1920).

XIII. *From the Hidden Way* (pub. 1916, rev. 1924) and *The Jewel Merchants* (pub. 1921): *Dizain and Comedy of Echoes.*

XIV. *The Rivet in Grandfather's Neck: A Comedy of Limitations* (pub. 1915).

XV. *The Eagle's Shadow: A Comedy of Purse-Strings* (pub. 1914, rev. 1923).

XVI. *The Cream of the Jest* (pub. 1917) and *The Lineage of Lichfield* (pub. 1922): *Two Comedies of Evasion.*

XVII.   *Straws and Prayer-Books: Dizain des Diversions* (pub. 1924).

XVIII.   *Townsend of Lichfield: Dizain des Adieux* (containing, in addition to the title piece and other odds and ends, *The White Robe* [pub. 1928], *The Way of Ecben* [pub. 1929], *Taboo* [pub. 1921], and *Sonnets from Antan* [pub. 1929]).

Preface to the Past. New York: Robert M. McBride & Company, 1936. (Reprints of prefaces to Storisende Edition, etc.)

The Witch-Woman: A Trilogy About Her. New York: Farrar, Straus and Company, 1948. (Reprints of *The Music from Behind the Moon, The Way of Ecben,* and *The White Robe.*)

B.   Later Essays and Autobiography

Some of Us: An Essay in Epitaphs. New York: Robert M. McBride & Company, 1930.

"Their Lives and Letters":

1. *These Restless Heads: A Trilogy of Romantics.* New York: Robert M. McBride & Company, 1932.
2. *Special Delivery: A Packet of Replies.* New York: Robert M. McBride & Company, 1933.
3. *Ladies and Gentlemen: A Parcel of Reconsiderations.* New York: Robert M. McBride & Company, 1934.

"Virginians are Various":

1. *Let Me Lie: Being in the Main an Ethnological Account of the Remarkable Commonwealth of Virginia and the Making of Its History.* New York: Farrar, Straus and Company, 1947.
2. *Quiet, Please.* Gainesville: University of Florida Press, 1952.
3. *As I Remember It: Some Epilogues in Recollection.* New York: The McBride Company, 1955.

C.   Later Predominantly Fictional Trilogies

"The Nightmare Has Triplets":

1. *Smirt: An Urbane Nightmare.* New York: Robert M. McBride & Company, 1934.
2. *Smith: A Sylvan Interlude.* New York: Robert M. McBride & Company, 1935.
3. *Smire: An Acceptance in the Third Person.* Garden City: Doubleday, Doran & Company, Inc., 1937.

"Heirs and Assigns":

1. *Hamlet Had an Uncle: A Comedy of Honor.* New York: Farrar & Rinehart, Inc., 1940.
2. *The King Was in His Counting House: A Comedy of Common-Sense.* New York: Farrar & Rinehart, 1938.
3. *The First Gentleman of America: A Comedy of Conquest.* New York: Farrar & Rinehart, Inc., 1942.

"It Happened in Florida":

1. *The St. Johns: A Parade of Diversities* (with A. J. Hanna). Rivers of America Series. New York: Farrar & Rinehart, Inc., 1943.
2. *There Were Two Pirates: A Comedy of Division.* New York: Farrar, Straus and Company, Inc., 1946.
3. *The Devil's Own Dear Son: A Comedy of the Fatted Calf.* New York: Farrar, Straus and Company, 1949.

SECONDARY SOURCES

BREWER, FRANCES JOAN. *James Branch Cabell: A Bibliography of His Writings, Biography and Criticism.* With a Foreword by James Branch Cabell. Charlottesville: University of Virginia Press, 1957. Extensive description of Cabell's published works; an invaluable listing of items about him.

BRUCCOLI, MATTHEW J. *James Branch Cabell: A Bibliography, Part II: Notes on the Cabell Collections at the University of Virginia.* Charlottesville: University of Virginia Press, 1957. Most of the manuscript letters described are to Guy Holt and Ellen Glasgow.

CARGILL, OSCAR. *Intellectual America: Ideas on the March.* New York: The Macmillan Company, 1941. Contains (pp. 495-503) probably the most destructive critique of Cabell.

HATCHER, HARLAN. "James Branch Cabell," *Creating the Modern American Novel.* New York: Farrar & Rinehart, 1935. A judicious appraisal of Cabell (pp. 191-201) as a romanticist in an age of realism.

HERGESHEIMER, JOSEPH. "James Branch Cabell," *The American Mercury,* XIII (January, 1928), 38-47. One of the best examples of the extravagant praise accorded Cabell in the later 1920's, somewhat before the Great Depression.

HIMELICK, RAYMOND. "Cabell, Shelley, and The 'Incorrigible Flesh,'" *The South Atlantic Quarterly,* XLVII (January, 1948), 88-95; "Figures of Cabell," *Modern Fiction Studies,* II (Winter, 1956-

57), 214-20; and "Cabell and the Modern Temper," *The South Atlantic Quarterly*, LVIII (Spring, 1959), 176-84. Brilliant revaluations stressing spirit of Swift and Voltaire.

HOWARD, LEON. "Figures of Allegory," *Sewanee Review*, XLII (January-March, 1934), 54-66. Penetrating analyses of pessimism in the major, cosmic comedies.

McNEILL, WARREN A. *Cabellian Harmonics*. With an Introductory Note by James Branch Cabell. New York: Random House, 1928. A pedestrian but valuable study of Cabell's uses of music and poetry.

PALMER, JOE H. "James Branch Cabell: Dualist," *Letters* (Lexington, Ky.), (February, 1929), 6-14. Condenses insights into Cabell's thought that are developed at greater length in Palmer's unpublished M.A. thesis, University of Kentucky, 1928. Cabell's letter to the author praising the article appears in *Letters* (May, 1929), 47.

PARKS, EDD WINFIELD. "James Branch Cabell." *Southern Renascence: The Literature of the Modern South*. Eds., Louis D. Rubin, Jr. and Robert D. Jacobs. Baltimore: The Johns Hopkins Press, 1953. Balanced revaluation of achievement (perverse humanism) and limitations (mannerism, etc.).

PARRINGTON, VERNON LOUIS. "The Incomparable Mr. Cabell." *The Beginnings of Critical Realism in America, Main Currents in American Thought*, III. New York: Harcourt, Brace and Company, 1930. This reprint of an article from *The Pacific Review* (December, 1921) reflects idolization of Cabell at the outset of the 1920's.

RUBIN, LOUIS D., JR. "Two in Richmond: Ellen Glasgow and James Branch Cabell." *South: Modern Southern Literature and Its Cultural Setting*. Eds. Louis D. Rubin, Jr. and Robert D. Jacobs. Garden City: Dolphin Books, Doubleday & Company, Inc., 1961.
————. "A Southerner in Poictesme." *No Place on Earth: Ellen Glasgow, James Branch Cabell And Richmond-in-Virginia*. Austin: University of Texas Press, 1959. These studies provide the basis for regarding Cabell as an allegorical regionalist with universal interests and values.

STEWART, DONALD OGDEN. "Cristofer Colombo: A Comedy of Discovery," *A Parody Outline of History*. Garden City: Garden City Publishing Co., Inc., 1921. An uproarious Cabell parody with considerable critical value.

VAN DOREN, CARL. *James Branch Cabell* (rev. ed.). New York: The Literary Guild, 1932. A dated but still valuable introduction.

WAGENKNECHT, EDWARD. "James Branch Cabell: The Anatomy of Romanticism." *Cavalcade of the American Novel*. New York:

Henry Holt and Company, 1952. The most informative, comprehensive, and sympathetic short introductory study.

WARD, CHRISTOPHER. "The Way of Cabelle: A Comedietta Involving a Transformation," *The Saturday Review of Literature*, VII (September 6, 1930), 102. Another parody with some critical value.

WELLS, ARVIN R. *Jesting Moses: A Study in Cabellian Comedy*. University of Michigan, unpublished Ph.D. dissertation, 1959. Uses Vaihinger and Santayana to clarify Cabell's world-view (pp. 13-46); devotes chapters to comic vision (pp. 38-46) and theory of comedy (pp. 47-101); and analyzes in detail the development of his comedy from the social to the cosmic (pp. 102-209). Eventually to be published by the University of Florida Press, this is an indispensable, advanced study.

WILSON, EDMUND. "The James Branch Cabell Case Reopened," *The New Yorker* (April 21, 1956), 129-56. The finest critical essay yet published.

Index

Cabell, John, 24
Cabell, Lizzie, 23
Cabell, Margaret Freeman (the second Mrs. James Branch Cabell), Preface, 19, 38, 41
Cabell, Priscilla Bradley (Mrs. Emmett A. Shepherd, later the first Mrs. James Branch Cabell), 17, 19, 34, 35, 36, 39, 40-41, 116
Cabell, Richard, 29, 131
Cabell, Robert Gamble I, 23
Cabell, Robert Gamble II, 23
Cabell, Robert Gamble III, 24
Cabell, William, Mrs., 32
Cabell, William H., 23
Caesar, Julius, 131
Carlyle, Thomas, 59
Carmer, Carl, 141
Carroll, Lewis, 133
Casanova, 33, 109
Cather, Willa, 129-30
Certain Measure, A (Glasgow), 130
Cervantes, 59
Chameleon (DeCasseres), 54-55
Chance (Conrad), 127
Chapelain, Jean, 131
Charlemagne, 66
Charles II of England, 32
Chivalrous attitude, defined, 46-47, 53, 66-87
Clark, Emily, 38
Clarke, Joseph H., 23
Clemens, S. L. (Mark Twain), Preface, 29, 132, 141
Clerici, Fabrizio, 132
Coleridge, S. T., 48, 126
Colum, Padriac, Preface
Comedic metaphor, 28, 53-57, 65, 141
"Comic Waste," 56-57, 141
Comstock, Anthony, 37
Confession, defined, 58
Congreve, William, 17, 27, 47, 55, 109, 122, 129
Conrad, Joseph, 59, 64, 126-27 131
Coolidge, Calvin, 75
Copernicus, 57, 60
Coriolanus (Shakespeare), 56
Coster, de, Charles, 48
Counterfeiters, The (Gide), 64

Cousins, Martha, 35
Crane, Stephen, 111, 142
Critical Approaches to Literature (Daiches), 129
Curious Myths of the Middle Ages (Baring-Gould), 60

Daiches, David, 129
Davis, Elmer, 39
Davis, Jefferson, 24
DeCasseres, Benjamin, 39, 54-55
Defore, Daniel, 57
Diabolism, defined, 28-30, 96, 99, 101, 109, 145
Dickens, Charles, 53, 131, 132, 144
Disney, Walt, 60
Dissertation Concerning the End for Which God Created the World (Edwards), 126
Döblin, Alfred, 64
Dolly Dialogues, The (Hope), 30
Don Juan (Byron), 37
Don Quixote (Cervantes), 59
Doré, Gustave, 24
Doubleday, Frank, Mrs., 37
Doyle, Arthur Conan, 29
Dreiser, Theodore, Preface, 27, 37, 39
Drew, Sarah, 121
Dumas, Alexandre, *père*, 131
Dunsany, Lord, 60

Edward I of England, 79, 80
Edward III of England, 80
Edwards, Jonathan, 126
Egoist, The (Meredith), 54
Endymion (Keats), 112
Egyptian Book of the Dead, 59
Emerson, R. W., 28
Epicoene (Jonson), 99
Erasmus, D., 58
Erewhon (Butler), 58
Etherege, George, 27, 55
Eusebius, 131

Faulkner, William, Preface, 29, 45, 46, 64, 94
Faustus, Johann, 131
Fielding, Henry, 53, 54, 57, 143
Finnegans Wake (Joyce), 59, 132-33